Knitting Simple Jackets

Knitting Simple Jackets
25 Beautiful Designs

Marilyn Saitz Cohen

LARK BOOKS

A Division of Sterling Publishing Co., Inc.

New York

Editor:
Linda Kopp

Technical Consultant:
Ellen Liberles

Art Director:
Stacey Budge

Cover Designer:
Barbara Zaretsky

Assistant Editor:
Susan Kieffer

Associate Art Director:
Shannon Yokeley

Assistant Art Director:
Lance Wille

Art Production Assistant:
Jeff Hamilton

Editorial Assistance:
Delores Gosnell

Illustrator:
Orrin Lundgren

Photographer:
Stewart O 'Sheilds

Dedication

To the memory of my loving
parents, Ida and Morris Saitz.
They would have been so proud.

Library of Congress Cataloging-in-Publication Data

Cohen, Marilyn Saitz.
  Knitting simple jackets : 25 beautiful designs / Marilyn Saitz Cohen.
      p. cm.
  Includes index.
  ISBN 1-57990-857-8 (hardcover)
  1. Knitting--Patterns. 2. Jackets. I. Title.
TT825.C634 2006
746.43'20432--dc22

10 9 8 7 6 5 4 3 2 1

First Edition

Published by Lark Books, A Division of
Sterling Publishing Co., Inc.
387 Park Avenue South, New York, N.Y. 10016

Text © 2006, Marilyn Saitz Cohen
Photography © 2006, Lark Books unless otherwise specified
Illustrations © 2006 Lark Books unless otherwise specified

Distributed in Canada by Sterling Publishing,
c/o Canadian Manda Group, 165 Dufferin Street
Toronto, Ontario, Canada M6K 3H6

Distributed in the United Kingdom by GMC Distribution Services,
Castle Place, 166 High Street, Lewes, East Sussex, England BN7 1XU

Distributed in Australia by Capricorn Link (Australia) Pty Ltd.,
P.O. Box 704, Windsor, NSW 2756 Australia

If you have questions or comments about this book, please contact:
Lark Books
67 Broadway
Asheville, NC 28801
(828) 253-0467

Manufactured in China

ISBN 13: 978-1-57990-857-7
ISBN 10: 1-57990-857-8

For information about custom editions, special sales, premium and corporate
purchases, please contact Sterling Special Sales Department at 800-805-5489
or specialsales@sterlingpub.com.

contents

Introduction

My passion for the art of knitting and

designing is limitless and never ending.

For all the hundreds of garments

I have designed, there are many

hundreds more waiting to be

discovered in my dreams, to be

brought to life with lovingly

chosen colors, textures, stitches,

and patterns, and knitted with the

most beautiful yarns I can find.

Here in this book you will find

25 of these discoveries.

Thoughtful Choices

MY VISION FOR THIS BOOK: simple elegant jackets. My challenge: design the most basic, easy to knit, luxurious, and flattering jackets possible. As the designs began to evolve, it became clear that there was a general theme with numerous subtle variations. Many of these jackets are based on the classic Chanel look—a collarless, subtly shaped, uncomplicated, and timeless style that is easily worn with a variety of tops and skirts, dresses, jeans, and pants. Your stitch, yarn, and finishing choices will define your jacket's style, so take time to give each careful consideration.

Choosing the Yarn

The exciting part of knitting begins with choosing your yarn. For example, the Chanel-style jacket is somewhat structured and requires a yarn with lots of body to help retain its shape as it is knit, assembled, and worn. You will see patterns in this book using a sturdy chenille, a tweed silk held double, a tightly woven mercerized Egyptian cotton, and a wide, strong, nylon ribbon.

In some of the softer, drapier styles, it works well to use light-weight yarn. A furry synthetic yarn is used in the Vintage Fur jacket, while an extra-fine merino yarn lends a luxurious feel to the project featured on the cover. A fine mohair provides the fluid look of The Big Wrap, and the delicate properties of a merino silk blend produces a smooth and lacy effect, as seen in the Long & Lacy project.

It is important to choose a good quality yarn for any of your projects, considering the time and effort involved. Most of these jackets are knitted with yarns especially blended for durability. They include combinations of fine merino and silk, cotton and linen, angora and wool, and cashmere and silk. A few of the designs, such as The Mandarin Jacket, called for some of my favorite luxury yarns—100% cashmere. I used pashmina cashmere and silk to create the Pashmina and Silk jacket, and 100% silk tweed for Tweed Chanel.

Choosing the Stitches

There is a welcome challenge to choosing the stitches for each yarn. It is always worth taking the time to make as many swatches as necessary in order to find the most pleasing stitch for the yarn, as well as the proper needle size and the correct gauge. Some of the yarns chosen for this book are so beautiful in texture and color, all that is needed is a basic stockinette or garter stitch to complement them and to enhance the beauty of the design. For example, the stockinette stitch is well suited for the silk tweed used in Tweed Chanel, as well as the crisp cotton-linen yarn in Elegant Kimono, and for showcasing the boldness of the thick and thin yarn in Clouds. I chose the garter stitch for Hooded Big Coat and the Sleeveless Jacket to help them maintain their body and shape.

Other yarns require simple patterns to best highlight their flexibility and richness. For example, I chose an easy two-row rib stitch pattern for a pashmina and silk combination to provide the jacket with comfort and stretch, whereas with the Shadow Cable jacket, a cable pattern best suited the design and yarn. In using a very fine merino-silk combination yarn, I found that a four-row lacy pattern on large needles worked well. The result is a modern, long, and intricately lacy jacket using an easy-to-follow traditional pattern. Stitch instructions are listed at the beginning of each pattern, making it handy if you're new to knitting or need a refresher course on a particular stitch.

Choosing the Style

Most of the jackets in this book are very simple in design so as to be flattering to most all who knit and wear them. Often, the shoulders are "dropped"—that is, without armhole shaping, so that the fit is casual and comfortable. Also, there is a minimum of traditional ribbing at the sleeve edges, and most are long enough to be worn cuffed.

The shaping of these jackets as well as the choice of stitch patterns is minimal and classic. This leaves room for your personal choice of closures and accent pieces, such as hand-crocheted or purchased buttons, a braided "frog," or a special coat pin you love.

Choosing the Finishing

One of my favorite finishings on many of these projects is the reverse single crochet. Wherever it is used, it provides a fine tailored finish to a classic look at the front, bottom, neckline, and sleeve cuff edges. Also, I like to use single crochet and slip stitch as finishings. However, I finished the edges of the Shadow Cable Jacket in an unusual way. The stitches are picked up all around the bottom, front, and neck edges with a circular needle, knitted for seven rows, bound off, and allowed to roll forward naturally for a contemporary, three-dimensional look.

Design
Considerations

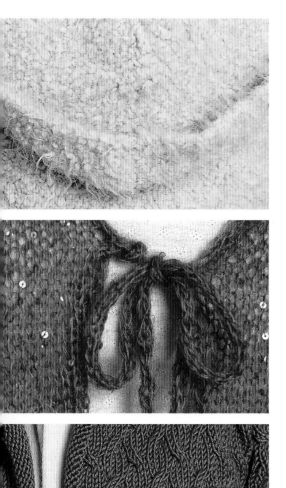

I DESIGNED MANY OF THE JACKETS IN THIS BOOK WITH the idea that by varying the color, yarn, and stitch choices, as well as lengths and finishings, each would look unique.

For some designs, I varied the basic style by adding a collar, a hood, crocheted or purchased buttons, or a frog closure. To others I added a tie belt or scarf, pockets, a mandarin collar, or funnel neck. The resulting styles are wide-ranging—from kimono to poncho, and from a long, light, wraparound to a tiny shoulder warmer. With a myriad of yarn choices in an endless color spectrum, and with the stitches and styles chosen to emphasize each design, creating the jackets was a constant pleasure...the discovery of what a jacket could be.

For me, there are three important components in designing knitwear that is appealing to most everybody.

My first consideration is the practical appeal. Will it fit properly? Are the yarns of fine quality? Will it stand up to a lot of wear? Is the style basic and timeless so that all the hours spent knitting will make it worthwhile and lasting? Is it fun to knit and can it be done in a reasonable amount of time? Are the instructions clear and precise?

Secondly is the emotional appeal. Do I love the feel of the yarn? Can it be knit for someone who will appreciate the special qualities of a handmade gift and the care taken with every stitch? Is it a satisfying project to me in all respects? Can I knit it for myself and be proud of it?

And thirdly is the artistic and creative appeal. Will the yarn chosen fit the style chosen? Does the yarn weight complement the design? Is the texture too soft, too bulky, too fine, too coarse, or perfectly matched? Does the color add to or subtract from the style? Is the stitch too intricate for the yarn, or would the yarn look better with a simpler presentation? Should the look be loose and flowing, or close to the body and more structured?

These are the questions I asked myself as the jackets in this book began to take on their individuality. Most of them are very easy or easy to knit and are labeled for level of ease, with only three in the intermediate range.

Now it's time for you to look through the projects, choose the one that appeals to you most, buy your yarn, and begin the simple pleasure of reaching for your needles and casting on! I believe you will find many jackets you will want to knit. I hope you enjoy your knitting adventure with this book as much as I enjoyed writing it.

In show-stopping red cashmere, this mandarin-collar jacket with side slits and a purchased frog closure at the neck is a timeless and easily knit design.

mandarin jacket

Experience Level
Easy

Sizes
Small, Medium, Large, X-Large

Finished Bust Measurements
39 (40½, 43, 44½)"/ 99 (103, 109, 113)cm
Standard Fit

Materials
Approx total: 845 (910, 975, 1040)yd/773 (832, 892, 951)m of cashmere bulky-weight yarn

Knitting needles: 6mm (size 10 U.S.) *or size to obtain gauge*

Crochet hook: 5.5mm (size I/9)

Tapestry needle for sewing seams

Gauge
14 sts and 18 rows = 4"/10cm in Stockinette Stitch

Always take time to check your gauge.

Pattern Stitch

Stockinette Stitch

Row 1 and all RS rows: Knit all stitches.

Row 2 and all WS rows: Purl all stitches.

Repeat rows 1 and 2 for pattern.

Instructions

BACK
With larger needles, cast on 66 (70, 74, 76) sts.

Work in Stockinette Stitch until piece measures 12 (13, 13½, 14)"/30.5 (33, 34, 35.5)cm from beginning.

Armhole shaping
Bind off 4 sts at beginning of next 2 rows.

Work even on 58 (62, 66, 68) sts until piece measures 20 (21, 22, 23)"/51 (53.5, 56, 58.5)cm from beginning.

Bind off all sts for shoulders and neck.

LEFT FRONT
With larger needles, cast on 36 (36, 38, 40) sts.

Work in Stockinette St until piece measures same as back to armholes.

Armhole shaping
At arm edge, bind off 4 sts once.

Work even on 32 (32, 34, 36) sts until armhole measures 6 (6, 6½, 7)"/ 15 (15, 16.5, 18)cm.

Neck shaping

At front edge, bind off 12 sts once. At same edge decrease 1 st every row 5 (3, 3, 4) times.

Work even on 15 (17, 19, 20) sts until piece measures same as back to shoulder shaping.

Bind off all stitches.

RIGHT FRONT

Work to correspond to left front, reversing all shaping.

SLEEVES

Make 2.

With larger needles, cast on 36 (36, 38, 40) sts

Work in Stockinette St, increasing 1 st each side every 7 (7, 7, 8) rows 12 times.

Work even on 60 (60, 62, 64) sts until sleeve measures 20 (20, 21, 22)"/51 (51, 53.5, 56)cm from beginning.

Bind off all sts.

FINISHING

Sew shoulder seams. Sew top edge of a sleeve to straight edge of each armhole; sew top side edge of sleeve to adjacent bound-off sts of armhole. Sew underarm and side seams, leaving a 2"/5cm slit opening at bottom of each side seam.

Collar

With smaller needles and right side of work facing you, pick up and knit sts around neck edge, spacing sts evenly to keep edges flat and smooth.

Starting on the wrong side with a purl row, work in Stockinette St for 2"/5cm, decreasing 1 st at each end of last row, then decrease again each end on the bind-off row.

Crocheted edging

With right side of work facing you, starting on bottom edge at right seam slit, crochet a row of single crochet (sc) around outer edge of jacket, including collar and working around to second slit at left seam. Leave slit edges unworked. Do not turn work, but work a row of reverse sc (see facing page) over sts just made back to starting point. Fasten off yarn and reattach to work a row of sc across bottom of back between slits; work a row of reverse sc over these sts and fasten off. Work sc and reverse sc rows around each sleeve edge.

Sew purchased frog closures onto fronts just below collar.

Reverse sc
A reverse sc is a single crochet st worked backwards from left to right (instead of right to left) as follows:

With right side of work facing you, insert hook from front to back into the next st to the right, yarn over and draw the yarn through the st, yarn over again and draw the yarn through both loops on the hook to complete the reverse sc.

THIS PROJECT WAS KNIT WITH 13 (14, 15, 16) balls of Classic Elite *Sinful*, 100% cashmere yarn, bulky weight, 1¾oz/50g = approx 65yd/59m per ball, color #92028.

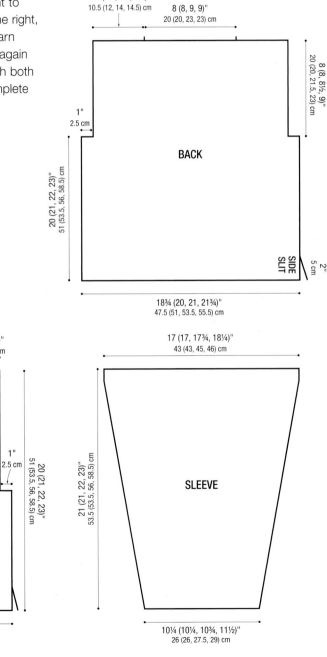

4¼ (4¾, 5½, 5¾)"
10.5 (12, 14, 14.5) cm

8 (8, 9, 9)"
20 (20, 23, 23) cm

8 (8, 8½, 9)"
20 (20, 21.5, 23) cm

1"
2.5 cm

BACK

20 (21, 22, 23)"
51 (53.5, 56, 58.5) cm

SIDE SLIT

2"
5 cm

18¾ (20, 21, 21¾)"
47.5 (51, 53.5, 55.5) cm

4¼ (4¾, 5½, 5¾)"
10.5 (12, 14, 14.5) cm

2"
5 cm

1"
2.5 cm

LEFT FRONT

20 (21, 22, 23)"
51 (53.5, 56, 58.5) cm

10¼ (10¼, 10¾, 11½)"
26 (26, 27.5, 29) cm

17 (17, 17¾, 18¼)"
43 (43, 45, 46) cm

SLEEVE

21 (21, 22, 23)"
53.5 (53.5, 56, 58.5) cm

10¼ (10¼, 10¾, 11½)"
26 (26, 27.5, 29) cm

You can knit this one-size-fits-all golden capelet in three easy pieces, using the simple stockinette stitch for the body and garter stitch for the border. There is a hidden hook-and-eye closing at the top.

dramatic
capelet

Experience Level
Easy

Size
One size fits all.

Finished Measurements
Circumference at lower edge,
   69"/175cm

Length, 24"/61cm

Materials
Approx total: Main color (MC):
   770yd/704m of cashmere and wool
   blend bulky-weight yarn

Contrasting color (CC): 216 yd/198m
   of polyamide eyelash-type bulky-
   weight yarn

Knitting needles: 6.5mm (size 10½ U.S.)
   or size to obtain gauge

Tapestry needle for sewing seams

Hook and eye

Gauge
14 sts and 18 rows = 4"/10cm in
   Stockinette Stitch

Always take time to check your gauge.

Pattern Stitches
Stockinette Stitch
Row 1 and all RS rows: Knit all stitches.

Row 2 and all WS rows: Purl all stitches.

Repeat rows 1 and 2 for pattern.

Garter Stitch
Knit every row.

Instructions

BACK
With contrasting color (CC), cast on 116 sts.

Work in Garter Stitch for 8 rows.

Change to main color (MC). Work in Stockinette Stitch and decrease 2 sts
(by working knit 3 together) each side every 5 rows 20 times. Work even on
36 sts until piece measures 24"/61cm from beginning.

Bind off all sts.

LEFT FRONT
With CC, cast on 64 sts.

Work in Garter St for 8 rows.

Change to MC and work in Stockinette St and at side (arm) edge, decrease
2 sts (knit 3 together) every 5 rows 20 times and at the same time when
piece measures 22¼"/56.5cm from beginning, shape neck.

Neck shaping
At front edge, bind off 6 sts every other row 4 times.

All sts should now be worked off.

Front border

Hold front sideways with right side facing you and front edge at top.

With CC, pick up about 78 sts along front edge between neck edge and bottom, spacing sts evenly to keep edge smooth and flat.

Work even in Garter St for 8 rows.

Bind off all sts.

RIGHT FRONT

Work to correspond to left front, reversing all shaping.

FINISHING

Sew side seams.

Neck trim

With right side of work facing you, using CC, pick up and knit 30 sts along right front neck edge, 36 sts across back neck, and 30 sts along left front neck edge for a total of 96 sts.

Work in Garter St as follows:

Row 1: *Knit 2, knit 2 together; repeat from * across (72 sts remain).

Rows 2 through 4: Knit all stitches.

Row 5: *Knit 4, knit 2 together; repeat from * across (60 sts remain).

Rows 6 through 8: Knit all stitches.

Bind off.

Sew hook and eye to fronts at top trim.

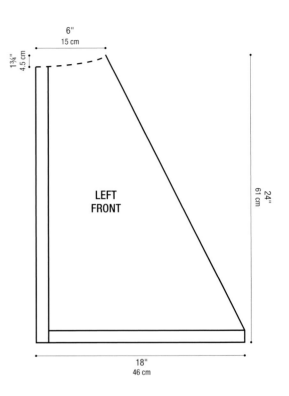

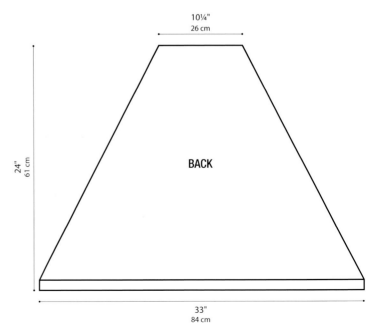

**THIS PROJECT
WAS KNIT WITH**
(MC) 10 balls of
Karabella Yarns *Margrite
Bulky*, 20% cashmere/80%
extra-fine merino wool yarn,
bulky weight, 1¾oz/50g =
approx 77yd/70m per ball, color
#M09, and (CC) 4 balls of Anny Blatt
Pollux, 100% polyamide fur-type yarn,
bulky weight, 1¾oz/50g = approx
54yd/49m per ball, color #383.

This stylish wraparound is simply a rectangle with sleeves. It can be worn many different ways: slipped on with one front tossed shawl-like over the opposite shoulder, open with both fronts draping softly, or held at the shoulder with a favorite pin.

versatile wrap

Experience Level
Easy

Size
One size fits all.

Finished Measurements
72" x 24"/183 x 61cm

Materials
Approx total: 1500yd/1372m of kid mohair, polyamide, and wool blend lightweight yarn

Knitting needles: 5mm (size 8 U.S.) and 6mm (size 10 U.S.) *or size to obtain gauge*

Tapestry needle for sewing seams

Gauge
18 sts and 22 rows = 4"/10cm in Stockinette Stitch

Always take time to check your gauge.

Pattern Stitches

Stockinette Stitch
Row 1 and all RS rows: Knit all stitches.

Row 1 and all WS rows: Purl all stitches.

Repeat rows 1 and 2 for pattern.

Rib Stitch
(multiple of 4 sts plus 2)

Row 1: Knit 2, *purl 2, knit 2; repeat from * across.

Row 2: Purl 2, *knit 2, purl 2; repeat from * across.

Repeat rows 1 and 2 for pattern.

Instructions

BODY
Note: Piece is worked from side to side.

With larger needles, loosely cast on 110 sts.

Work in Stockinette Stitch until piece measures 26"/66cm from beginning, ending with a purl row.

First armhole
On next row, knit 20, tightly bind off next 30

sts for armhole, knit the remaining 60 sts.

On the following row, purl 60, cast on 30 sts over those bound-off, purl remaining 20 sts.

Continue in Stockinette St on 110 sts for another 20"/51cm, ending with a purl row.

Second armhole

Work next 2 rows same as for first armhole.

Continue in Stockinette St on 110 sts for another 26"/66cm, for a total length of 72"/183cm from beginning.

Bind off all sts.

SLEEVES

Note: Sleeves are designed to fit very closely. The yarn used for this garment was quite stretchy. If you substitute a different yarn, be sure to check, after working several rows, that the cast-on edge will fit over your hand. If you need to, use larger needles to cast on and work beginning rows.

Make 2.

With smaller needles, loosely cast on 26 sts.

Work in Rib Stitch and keeping continuity of pattern as established, increase 1 st each side every 5 rows 26 times.

Work even on 78 sts until sleeve measures 24"/61cm.

Bind off all sts loosely.

FINISHING

Sew the sleeve seams. Fit sleeves into armholes, with seam at bottom, and sew in place. Edges of wrap will roll gently.

THIS PROJECT WAS KNIT WITH 10 balls of Muench GGH *Soft Kid*, 70% super kid mohair/25% polyamide/5% wool yarn, lightweight, .88oz/25g = approx 150yd/137m per ball, color #027.

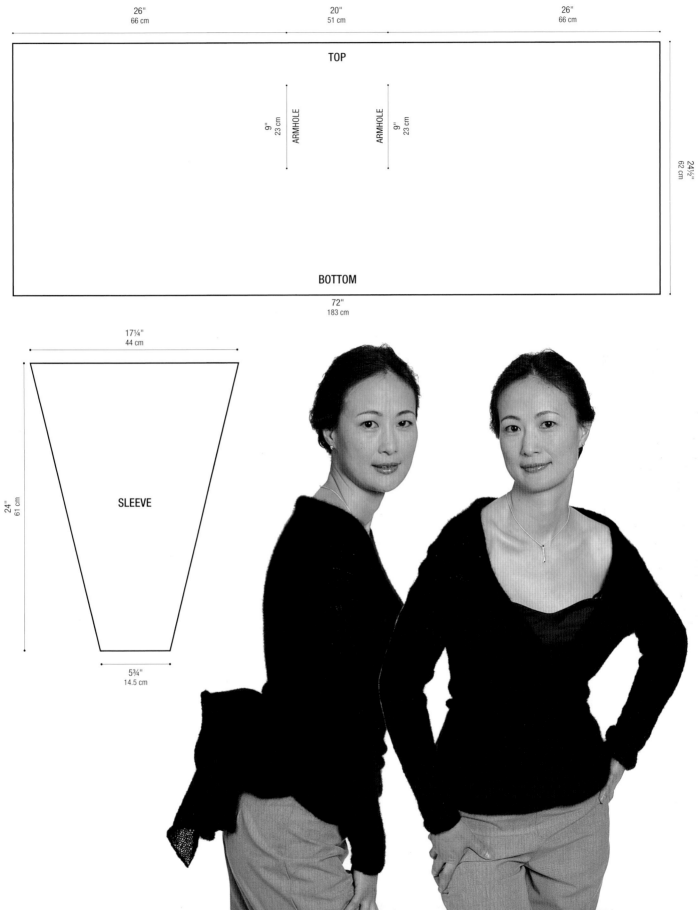

26"
66 cm

20"
51 cm

26"
66 cm

TOP

9"
23 cm

ARMHOLE

ARMHOLE

9"
23 cm

24½"
62 cm

BOTTOM

72"
183 cm

17¼"
44 cm

SLEEVE

24"
61 cm

5¾"
14.5 cm

simple cardigan

What makes this basic style unusual is the texture of the stitch. It's called the bat stitch—a very easy, two-row pattern used throughout the knitting. A soft, angora blend yarn reveals the texture in a subtle way. The only finishing is a crocheted slip stitch around the edges.

Experience Level
Easy

Sizes
Small, Medium/Large, X-Large

Finished Bust Measurements
39 (43, 47)"/99 (109, 119.5)cm
    Standard Fit

Materials
Approx total: 1364 (1488, 1612)yd/1247
    (1361, 1474)m of angora and wool
    blend medium-weight yarn

Knitting needles: 6.5mm (size 10½ U.S.)
    or size to obtain gauge

Crochet hook: 3.75mm (size F/5)

Tapestry needle for sewing seams

Gauge
18 sts and 28 rows = 4"/10cm in
    pattern

Always take time to check your gauge.

Pattern Stitches

Bat Stitch

(multiple of 3 sts plus 1)

Row 1 (RS): Knit all stitches.

Row 2: Knit 1, *keeping yarn in back of work slip 2 purlwise, knit 1; repeat from * across.

Repeat rows 1 and 2 for pattern.

Instructions

BACK

Cast on 85 (94, 103) sts.

Work in Bat Stitch pattern until piece measures 20 (21, 22)"/51 (53.5, 56)cm from beginning.

Bind off all sts from shoulders and neck.

LEFT FRONT

Cast on 46 (49, 55) sts.

Work in pattern until piece measures same as back to shoulders.

Bind off all sts.

THIS PROJECT WAS KNIT WITH 11 (12, 13) balls of Classic Elite *Lush*, 50% angora/50% wool yarn, medium weight, 1¾oz/50g = approx 124yd/113m per ball, color #4401.

RIGHT FRONT

Work same as for left front.

SLEEVES

Make 2.

Cast on 40 (43, 46) sts.

Work in pattern, increasing 1 st each side every 7 rows 16 (17, 18) times. Work even on 72 (77, 82) sts until sleeve measures 19 (19, 20)"/48 (48, 51)cm.

Bind off all sts.

FINISHING

Starting from arm edge, sew shoulder seams, leaving about 4"/10cm free at each front neck edge to turn back for lapels. Mark side edges of fronts and back 8 (8½, 9)"/20 (21.5, 23)cm below shoulder seams for armholes. Sew top edge of a sleeve to each side between markers. Sew underarm and side seams, leaving a 2"/5cm slit opening at the bottom of each side seam.

Crocheted edging

With crochet hook, work a row of slip stitches all around outer edge of jacket, omitting slit edges. Fasten off when you come to a slit and reattach yarn on the other side to continue.

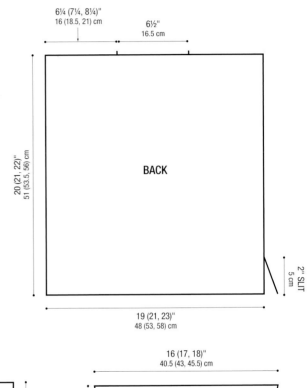

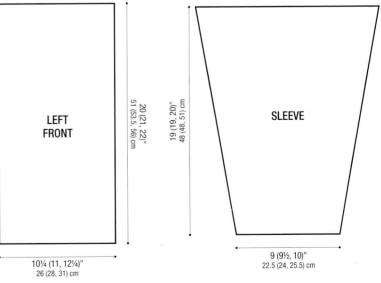

Tweedy, cozy, and colorful, this coat

is a pleasure to wear. The yarn

is held triple, and knits up

very quickly on large

needles. A long,

thickly-fringed

scarf will keep you

snug and stylish,

and you have a

choice of finishing

your jacket with

either a collar, as shown

in the photo, or a hood.

comfy car coat

Experience Level
Easy

Sizes
Small, Medium/Large, X-Large

Finished Bust Measurements
44 (50, 54)"/112 (127, 137)cm
   Loose Fit

Materials
Approx total: 2180 (2616,
   3052)yd/1993 (2392, 2791)m of
   wool medium-weight yarn. If you plan
   to make the hood rather than the collar, add another 109yd/100m to the
   total amount of yarn needed.

Knitting needles: 9mm (size 13 U.S.) for
   jacket or size to obtain gauge

Knitting needles: 5mm (size 8 U.S.) for
   scarf or size to obtain gauge

Crochet hook: 5.5mm (size I/9) for
   jacket and scarf

Tapestry needle for sewing seams

Gauge
8 sts and 14 rows = 4"/10cm in
   Stockinette Stitch for jacket

18 sts and 24 rows = 4"/10cm in
   Stockinette Stitch for scarf

Always take time to check your gauge.

Pattern Stitches
Stockinette Stitch
Row 1 and all RS rows: Knit all stitches.

Row 2 and all WS rows: Purl all stitches.

Repeat rows 1 and 2 for pattern.

Rib Stitch
(uneven number of sts)

Row 1 (wrong side): Purl 1, *knit 1, purl 1; repeat from * across.

Row 2: Knit 1, *purl 1, knit 1; repeat from * across.

Repeat rows 1 and 2 for pattern.

Instructions

BACK
With 3 strands of yarn held together and using larger needles, cast on 44 (48, 52) sts.

Work in Stockinette Stitch until piece measures 11 (13, 14)"/28 (33, 35.5)cm from beginning.

Armhole shaping
Bind off 3 sts at beginning of next 2 rows.

Work even on 38 (42, 46) sts until piece measures 22 (23, 24)"/56 (58.5, 61)cm from beginning.

Bind off all sts for shoulders and neck.

LEFT FRONT
With 3 strands of yarn and larger needles, cast on 22 (25, 28) sts.

Work in Stockinette St until piece measures same as back to armholes.

Armhole shaping
At arm edge, bind off 3 sts once.

Work even on 19 (22, 25) sts until piece measures 20 (21, 22)"/51 (53, 56)cm from beginning.

Neck shaping

At front edge, bind off 3 (3, 4) sts every other row twice. Decrease 1 st at same edge every row 2 (3, 2) times.

Work even, if needed, on 11 (13, 15) sts until piece measures same as back to shoulder.

Bind off all sts.

RIGHT FRONT

Work to correspond to left front, reversing all shaping.

SLEEVES

Make 2.

With 3 strands of yarn and larger needles, cast on 24 sts.

Work in Stockinette St and increase 1 st each side every 8 (7, 7) rows 8 (9, 10) times.

Work even on 40 (42, 44) sts until sleeve measures 20 (21, 22)"/51 (53.5, 56)cm from beginning.

Bind off all sts.

COLLAR

Sew shoulder seams, using 3 strands of yarn.

With right side of work facing you, using 3 strands of yarn and larger needles, pick up and knit 16 sts along right neck edge, 17 sts across back neck, and 16 sts along left front neck edge.

Work in Rib Stitch on these 49 sts for 6"/15cm.

Bind off all sts in pattern.

HOOD

Sew shoulder seams, using 3 strands of yarn.

With right side of work facing you, using 3 strands of yarn and larger needles, pick up 16 sts along right front neck edge, 16 sts across back neck edge, and 16 sts from left front neck edge, for a total of 48 sts.

Starting on wrong side with a purl row, work in Stockinette St and decrease 1 st each side edge every 14 rows 4 times and at the same time, when hood measures 11"/28cm from beginning at neck edge, form center top split as follows:

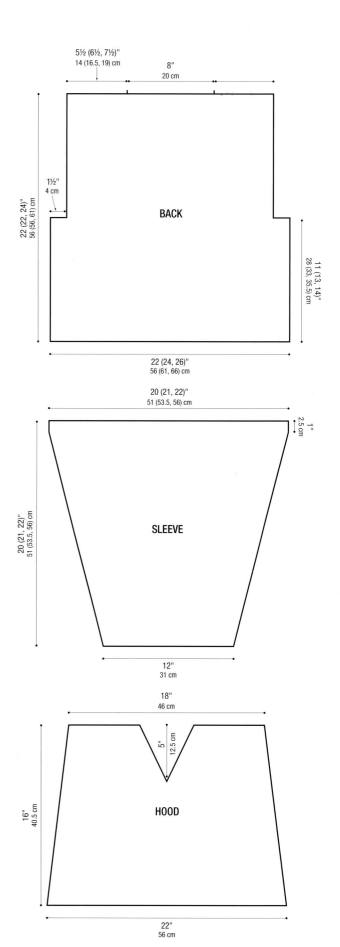

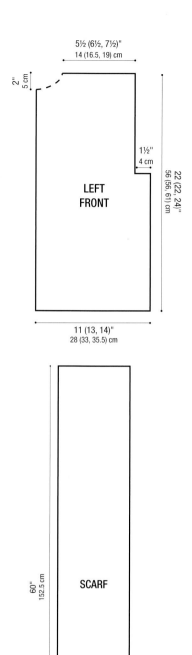

5½ (6½, 7½)"
14 (16.5, 19) cm

2"
5 cm

1½"
4 cm

LEFT FRONT

22 (22, 24)"
56 (56, 61) cm

11 (13, 14)"
28 (33, 35.5) cm

60"
152.5 cm

SCARF

10"
25.5 cm

On next row, work halfway across row, attach 3 new balls of yarn and with new yarn, complete row. Work each side separately with its own yarn, continuing to decrease at outer edge as before and decrease 1 st at each split edge every 4 rows 4 times. Work until hood measures 16"/40.5cm from neck edge.

Bind off all sts on each side.

Matching split and bound-off edges on one side to those on other side, sew center top seam.

SCARF

With single strand of yarn and using smaller needles, cast on 46 sts.

Work in Stockinette St until piece measures 60"/152.5cm.

Bind off all sts.

Fringes

For each fringe, cut six 14"/35.5cm strands. Fold group of strands in half and with crochet hook, draw the folded end through the scarf end from front to back to form a loop. Draw cut ends of strands through the loop and pull them gently to tighten the knot.

Make 9 fringes evenly spaced along each narrow end of scarf.

FINISHING

Sew all seams with 3 strands of yarn. Sew top edge of a sleeve to straight edge of each armhole, sewing top side edge of sleeve to adjacent bound-off sts of armhole. Sew underarm and side seams.

Crocheted edging

With crochet hook, starting on bottom edge at right seam, crochet a row of single crochet (sc) all around outer edge of coat, including collar or hood, spacing sts to keep edges flat and smooth. Repeat around each sleeve.

THIS PROJECT, WITH COLLAR, WAS KNIT WITH 20 (24, 28) balls, or with hood, 21 (25, 29) balls of Debbie Bliss *Aran Tweed*, 100% wool yarn, medium weight, 1¾oz/50g = approx 109yd/100m per ball, color #20001.

The fashionable stand-up

collar on this mini-jacket

commands attention

while warming your

neck, shoulders, and

arms in downy fur.

Use a #17

needle

and

three

strands of

yarn held together

to quickly knit one in any

color you choose.

mini-jacket

Experience Level
Easy

Sizes
Small, Medium/Large, X-Large

Finished Bust Measurements
36½ (40, 45)"/92.5 (101.5, 114.5)cm
  Close Fit

Materials
Approx total: 994 (1136, 1278)yd/909
  (1039, 1169)m of polyamide nylon
  medium-weight yarn

Knitting needles: 12.75mm (size 17
  U.S.) *or size to obtain gauge*

Crochet hook: 6.5mm (size K/10)

Tapestry needle for sewing seams

Gauge
6 sts and 9 rows = 4"/10cm in
  Stockinette Stitch

Always take time to check your gauge.

Pattern Stitches
Stockinette Stitch
Row 1 and all RS rows: Knit all stitches.

Row 2 and all WS rows: Purl all stitches.

Repeat rows 1 and 2 for pattern.

Rib Stitch
(multiple of 2 sts plus 1)

Row 1: Knit 1, *purl 1, knit 1; repeat from * across.

Row 2: Purl 1, *knit 1, purl 1; repeat from * across.

Repeat rows 1 and 2 for pattern.

Instructions

BACK
With 3 strands of yarn held together, cast on 28 (30, 34) sts.

Work in Stockinette Stitch until piece measures 14 (14, 15)"/35.5 (35.5, 38)cm from beginning.

Shoulder shaping
Bind off 8 (9, 11) sts at beginning of next 2 rows.

Place remaining 12 sts at center on a holder for collar.

LEFT FRONT

With 3 strands of yarn held together, cast on 14 (16, 18) sts.

Work in Stockinette St until piece measures same as back to shoulder.

Shoulder shaping

At arm edge, bind off 8 (9, 11) sts once.

Place remaining 6 (7, 7) sts on a holder for collar.

RIGHT FRONT

Work to correspond to left front, reversing shaping.

SLEEVES

Make 2.

With 3 strands of yarn held together, cast on 14 (14, 16) sts.

Work in Stockinette St, increasing 1 st each side on fifth row, then every 9 (7, 7) rows thereafter 3 (4, 4) times more.

Work even on 22 (24, 26) sts until sleeve measures 16 (16, 17)"/40.5 (40.5, 43)cm from beginning.

Bind off all sts.

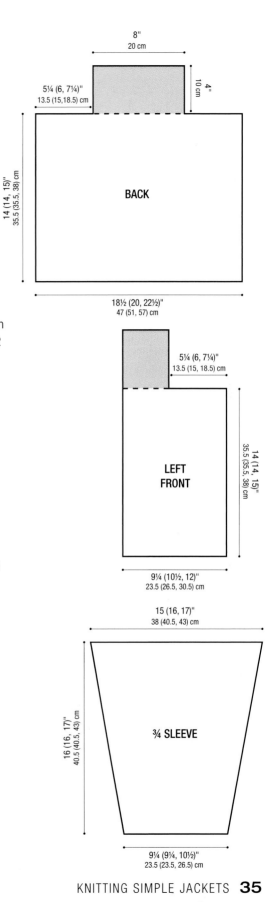

8"
20 cm

5¼ (6, 7¼)"
13.5 (15,18.5) cm

4"
10 cm

BACK

14 (14, 15)"
35.5 (35.5, 38) cm

18½ (20, 22½)"
47 (51, 57) cm

5¼ (6, 7¼)"
13.5 (15, 18.5) cm

LEFT FRONT

14 (14, 15)"
35.5 (35.5, 38) cm

9¼ (10½, 12)"
23.5 (26.5, 30.5) cm

15 (16, 17)"
38 (40.5, 43) cm

¾ SLEEVE

16 (16, 17)"
40.5 (40.5, 43) cm

9¼ (9¼, 10½)"
23.5 (23.5, 26.5) cm

FINISHING

Sew shoulder seams.

Collar

With right side of work facing you, pick up and knit 6 (7, 7) sts from right front holder, pick up 1 st from shoulder seam area, then 12 sts from back holder, and 6 (7, 7) sts from left front holder.

Work these 25 (27, 27) sts in Rib Stitch for 4"/10cm.

Bind off all sts in ribbing.

Mark side edges of fronts and back 7½ (8, 8½)"/19 (20, 21.5)cm below shoulder seams for armholes. Sew top edge of a sleeve to each side between markers. Sew underarm and side seams.

Crocheted edging

With right side of work facing you, crochet a row of single crochet (sc) all around outer edges of jacket body, spacing sts to keep edges flat and smooth. Crochet around each sleeve edge in same manner.

THIS PROJECT WAS KNIT WITH 14 (16, 18) balls of Muench GGH *Amelie*, 100% polyamide nylon yarn, medium weight, 1¾oz/50g = 71yd/65m per ball, color #12.

Knit in an easy-to-follow, four-row pattern called "fern lace," this graceful, light-weight coat is destined to become a cherished favorite. The beauty of the lace, simplicity of the style, and the fine quality of the yarn make this project well worth the knitting time.

long & lacy

Experience Level

Intermediate

Sizes

Small/Medium, Large/X-Large

Finished Bust Measurements

Approx 39 (46)"/99 (117)cm
   Standard Fit

Materials

Approx total: 2353 (2896)yd/2152
   (2648)m of merino wool and silk
   blend lightweight yarn

Knitting needles: 4mm (size 6 U.S.)
   or size to obtain gauge

Crochet hook: 3.5mm (size E/4)

Tapestry needle for sewing seams

Gauge

26 sts and 26 rows = 4"/10cm in
   pattern

Always take time to check your gauge.

Pattern Stitch

Fern Lace
(multiple of 9 sts plus 4)

Row 1 (wrong side): Purl all stitches.

Row 2: Knit 3, *yarn over, knit 2, slip 1, knit 1, pass slipped stitch over (psso), knit 2 together, knit 2, yarn over, knit 1; repeat from * across to last stitch, knit 1.

Row 3: Purl all stitches.

Row 4: Knit 2, *yarn over, knit 2, slip 1, knit 1, psso, knit 2 together, knit 2, yarn over, knit 1; repeat from * across to last 2 sts, knit 2.

Repeat rows 1 through 4 for pattern.

Instructions

BACK

Cast on 148 (166) sts.

Work in Fern Lace pattern and, keeping continuity of pattern as established, decrease 1 st each side every 38 (46) rows 6 (5) times.

Work even on 136 (156) sts until piece measures 36"/91.5cm from beginning.

Bind off all sts for shoulders and neck.

LEFT FRONT

Cast on 85 (103) sts.

Work in pattern and, leaving front edge straight, decrease 1 st at side edge, every 6 rows 26 times, then every 6 (5) rows 13 (15) times more.

Work even, if needed, on 46 (62) sts until piece measures same length as back to shoulder.

Bind off all sts.

RIGHT FRONT
Work to correspond to left front, reversing shaping.

SLEEVES
Make 2.

Cast on 58 (67) sts.

Work in pattern and, keeping continuity of pattern as established, increase 1 st at each side every 5 rows 20 times, then every 5 (4) rows 5 (7) times more.

Work even on 108 (121) sts until sleeve measures 20"/51cm from beginning.

Bind off all sts.

BELT
Cast on 22 sts.

Work in pattern until belt measures 58"/147cm from beginning.

Bind off.

FINISHING
Sew shoulder seams. Make side edges of front and back 8¼ (9¼)"/21 (23.5)cm below shoulder seams for armholes. Sew top edge of a sleeve to each side between markers. Sew underarm and side seams, easing edges to fit smoothly.

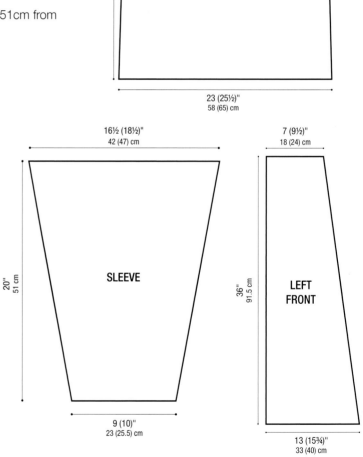

Crocheted edging

With right side of work facing you, starting on bottom edge at right seam, crochet a row of single crochet (sc) all around outer edge of coat, spacing stitches to keep edges smooth and flat. Work around to the starting point, then without turning, work a row of reverse sc (see below) over sts just made, working just loosely enough to keep edge smooth.

Reverse sc

A reverse sc is a single crochet st worked backwards from left to right (instead of right to left) as follows:

With right side of work facing you, insert hook from front to back into the next st to the right, yarn over and draw the yarn through the st, yarn over again and draw the yarn through both loops on the hook to complete the reverse sc.

Work this same sc and reverse sc edging around each sleeve edge.

Belt

Fold belt in half lengthwise; sew each end closed and long edges together with tiny overcast stitches (see Design Tip).

Design Tip

To work overcast stitches, thread yarn in a tapestry needle. Working from right to left, make tiny diagonal stitches over the edges, keeping the stitches evenly spaced and evenly sized.

THIS PROJECT WAS KNIT WITH 13 (16) balls of Grignasco *Champagne*, 75% merino wool/25% silk yarn, lightweight, 1 3/4oz/50g = approx 181yd/166m per ball, color #002.

Luxurious cashmere

and lustrous silk are

combined into one

yarn and knitted here

in a simple rib stitch.

This loose-fitting,

comfortable jacket

has deep pockets, a stylish,

drapey hood, and sleeves

long enough to be cuffed.

cashmere & silk

Experience Level
Easy

Sizes
Small, Medium/Large, X-Large

Finished Bust Measurements
43 (45¼, 47½)"/109 (115, 120.5)cm
Loose Fit

Materials
Approx total: 2090 (2200,
2310)yd/1911 (2012, 2112)m of
cashmere and silk blend medium-
weight yarn

Knitting needles: 6mm (size 10 U.S.) *or
size to obtain gauge*

Tapestry needle for sewing seams

Gauge
22 sts and 22 rows = 4"/10cm in Rib
Stitch

Always take time to check your gauge.

Pattern Stitch
Rib Stitch
(even number of sts)

Row 1: Knit 1, *knit 1, purl 1; repeat from * across to last st, knit 1.

Repeat row 1 for pattern.

Instructions

BACK
Cast on 116 (122, 130) sts.

Work in Rib Stitch pattern until piece measures 27 (27, 28)"/68.5 (68.5, 71)cm from beginning.

Bind off all sts in pattern for shoulders and neck.

LEFT FRONT
Cast on 60 (64, 66) sts.

Work in pattern until piece measures 24½ (24½, 25½)"/62 (62, 64.5)cm from beginning.

Neck shaping
At neck edge, bind off 9 (10, 8) sts once. At same edge, decrease 1 st every row 12 times.

Work even, if needed, on 39 (42, 46) sts until piece measures same as back to shoulder.

Bind off all sts in pattern.

RIGHT FRONT
Work to correspond to left front, reversing shaping.

SLEEVES

Make 2.

Cast on 60 (62, 66) sts.

Work in pattern for 4"/10cm. Continue in pattern and increase 1 st each side on next row, then every 4 rows 18 (20, 21) times, keeping continuity of pattern as established.

Work even on 98 (104, 110) sts until sleeve measures 19 (19½, 20)"/48 (49.5, 51)cm from beginning.

Bind off all sts in pattern.

POCKETS

Make 2.

Cast on 38 sts.

Work in pattern for 7"/18cm.

Bind off all sts in pattern.

FINISHING

Sew shoulder seams. Mark side edges of fronts and back 9 (9½, 10)"/23 (24, 25.5)cm below shoulder seams for armhole. Sew top edge of a sleeve to each side between markers. Sew underarm and side seams.

Hood

With right side of work facing you, pick up and knit 122 sts evenly spaced around neck edge. Work in Rib St pattern and decrease 1 st at each edge every 9 rows 9 times, and at same time when piece measures 11"/28cm from neck edge, form center split as follows:

On next row, work halfway across, attach a new ball of yarn and with new yarn, complete row. Work each side separately with its own yarn, continuing decreases at outer edges as before, and decrease 1 st at each split edge every 4 rows 6 times. Work until hood measures 16"/40.5cm from neck edge.

Bind off all remaining sts on each side.

Matching split and bound-off edges of one side to those on opposite side, sew center top seam of hood.

Sew a pocket to each front, positioning it 3"/7.5cm in from side seam and 1"/2.5cm above bottom edge.

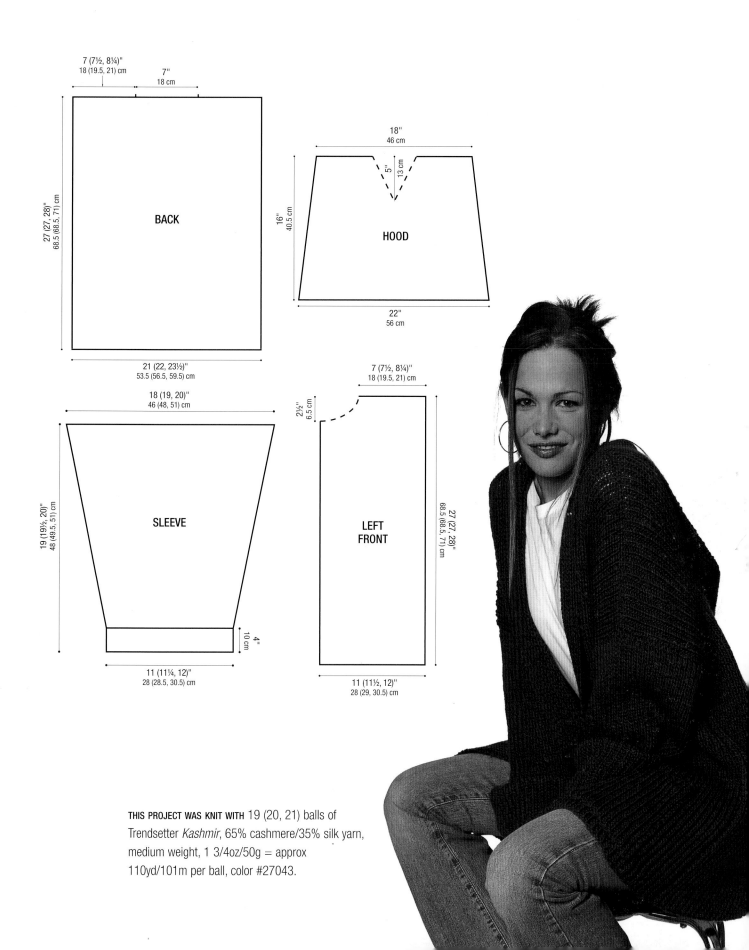

7 (7½, 8¼)"
18 (19.5, 21) cm

7"
18 cm

27 (27, 28)"
68.5 (68.5, 71) cm

BACK

21 (22, 23½)"
53.5 (56.5, 59.5) cm

18"
46 cm

5"
13 cm

16"
40.5 cm

HOOD

22"
56 cm

18 (19, 20)"
46 (48, 51) cm

19 (19½, 20)"
48 (49.5, 51) cm

SLEEVE

4"
10 cm

11 (11¼, 12)"
28 (28.5, 30.5) cm

7 (7½, 8¼)"
18 (19.5, 21) cm

2½"
6.5 cm

27 (27, 28)"
68.5 (68.5, 71) cm

LEFT
FRONT

11 (11½, 12)"
28 (29, 30.5) cm

THIS PROJECT WAS KNIT WITH 19 (20, 21) balls of
Trendsetter *Kashmir*, 65% cashmere/35% silk yarn,
medium weight, 1 3/4oz/50g = approx
110yd/101m per ball, color #27043.

classic chanel

A contemporary Chanel-style jacket is interpreted

here in a chunky and velvety, chenille yarn. Its

simplicity works beautifully with jeans, skirts, or

dressy evening wear. At two stitches to the inch,

you can finish it in a weekend.

Experience Level
Very Easy

Sizes
Small, Medium, Large, X-Large

Finished Bust Measurements
36 (38, 40, 42)"/91.5 (96.5, 101.5,
  106.5)cm
  Standard Fit

Materials
Approx total: 500 (600, 700, 800)yd/457
  (549, 640, 732)m acrylic and rayon
  chenille bulky-weight yarn

Knitting needles: 8mm (size 11 U.S.)
  or size to obtain gauge

Crochet hook: 5.5mm (size I/9)

Tapestry needle for sewing seams

Gauge
8 sts and 14 rows = 4"/10cm in
  Stockinette Stitch

Always take time to check your gauge.

Pattern Stitch

Stockinette Stitch

Row 1 and all RS rows: Knit all stitches.

Row 2 and all WS rows: Purl all stitches.

Repeat rows 1 and 2 for pattern.

Instructions

BACK

Cast on 36 (38, 40, 42) sts.

Work in Stockinette Stitch until piece measures 13 (13, 13½, 14)"/33 (33, 34, 35.5)cm from beginning.

Armhole shaping

Bind off 2 sts at the beginning of the next 2 rows.

Work even on 32 (34, 36, 38) sts until armhole measures 8 (8, 8½, 9)"/20 (20, 21.5, 23)cm.

Bind off all sts for shoulders and neck.

LEFT FRONT

Cast on 18 (19, 20, 21) sts.

Work in Stockinette St until piece measures same as back to armholes.

Armhole shaping

At arm edge, bind off 2 sts once.

Work even on 16 (17, 18, 19) sts until armhole measures 6 (6, 6 1/2, 7)"/15 (15, 16.5, 18)cm.

Neck shaping

At neck edge, bind off 6 (6, 7, 7) sts. Decrease 1 st at same edge every row twice.

Work even on 8 (9, 9, 10) sts until piece measures same as back to shoulder.

Bind off all sts.

THIS PROJECT WAS KNIT WITH 5 (6, 7, 8) balls of Lion Brand *Chenille Thick and Quick*, 91% acrylic/9% rayon chenille, bulky-weight yarn, 10oz/300g = approx 100yd/91m per ball, color #153 (black).

RIGHT FRONT

Work to correspond to left front, reversing all shaping.

SLEEVES

Sew shoulder seams.

With right side of work facing you, pick up and knit 30 (32, 34, 36) sts evenly spaced along one straight armhole edge.

Beginning with a purl row on wrong side, continue in Stockinette St and decrease as follows:

For Small and Medium sizes only, decrease 1 st each side every 14 rows 4 times.

For Large and X-Large sizes only, decrease 1 st each side every 12 rows 5 times.

For all sizes, work even on 22 (24, 24, 26) sts until sleeve measures 18½ (19, 19½, 20)"/47 (48, 49.5, 51)cm from beginning of armhole edge.

Bind off all sts.

Repeat for other sleeve.

FINISHING

Sew underarm and side seams.

Crocheted edging

With crochet hook, beginning on bottom edge at right seam, work a row of single crochet (sc) all around the outer edges of the jacket body, working 3 sc all in the same corner st to work around each lower front corner, and spacing sts to keep edges flat and smooth. When you work around to the starting point, begin working reverse sc (see Design Tip) over sts just made, working just loosely enough to keep edge smooth.

Work this same sc and reverse sc edging around each sleeve edge.

Design Tip

A reverse sc is a single crochet st worked backwards from left to right (instead of right to left) as follows:
With right side of work facing you, insert hook from front to back into the next st to the right, yarn over and draw the yarn through the st, yarn over again and draw the yarn through both loops on the hook to complete the reverse sc.

BACK

8 (8, 9, 9)"
20 (20, 23, 23) cm

4 (4½, 4½, 5)"
10.5 (11.5, 11.5, 12.5) cm

8 (8, 8½, 9)"
20 (20, 21.5, 23) cm

1"
(2.5 cm)

21 (21, 22, 23)"
53 (53, 56, 58.5) cm

13 (13, 13½, 14)"
33 (33, 34, 35.5) cm

18 (19, 20, 21)"
46 (48, 51, 53) cm

LEFT FRONT

4 (4½, 4½, 5)"
10.5 (11.5, 11.5, 12.5) cm

2"
5 cm

1"
(2.5 cm)

21 (21, 22, 23)"
53 (53, 56, 58.5) cm

9 (9½, 10, 10½)"
23 (24, 25.5, 28) cm

SLEEVE

15 (16, 17, 18)"
38 (40.5, 43, 45.5) cm

18½ (19, 19½, 20)"
47 (48, 49.5, 51) cm

11 (12, 12, 13)"
28 (30.5, 30.5, 33) cm

...is worked with a

...natte, ribbon-like yarn

...inish looks and feels

...e is timeless.

Pattern Stitches

Stockinette Stitch

Row 1 and all RS rows: Knit all stitches.

Row 2 and all WS rows: Purl all stitches.

Repeat rows 1 and 2 for pattern.

Garter Stitch

Knit every row.

Instructions

BACK

With 2 strands of yarn held together, cast on 60 (63, 66) sts.

Work in Garter Stitch for 2"/5cm.

Work in Stockinette Stitch until piece measures 21 (22, 23)"/53 (56, 58)cm from beginning.

Bind off all sts for shoulders and neck.

Experience Level
Easy

Sizes
Small, Medium/Large, X-Large

Finished Bust Measurements
41 (43, 46)"/104 (109, 117)cm
Standard Fit

Materials
Approx total: 2142 (2394, 2646)yd/1959 (2189, 2420)m polyamide nylon medium-weight yarn, held double throughout

Knitting needles: 6.5mm (size 10½ U.S.) *or size to obtain gauge*

Tapestry needle for sewing seams

Gauge
12 sts and 20 rows = 4"/10cm in Stockinette Stitch

Always take time to check your gauge.

LEFT FRONT

With yarn held double, cast on 32 (34, 36) sts.

Work in Garter St for 2"/5cm.

Next row (RS): Knit to last 7 sts at center front edge, place marker on needle, knit 7 for front border.

Following row: Knit 7, slip marker, purl 25 (27, 29) sts.

Continuing to work 7 sts at front edge in Garter St, work remaining sts in Stockinette St until piece measures 19 (20, 21)"/48 (51, 53.5)cm.

Neck shaping

At front edge, bind off 3 (4, 4) sts once, then 3 sts every other row twice. Decrease 1 st at same edge every row 3 times.

Bind off remaining 20 (21, 23) sts for shoulder.

RIGHT FRONT

Work same as left front until Garter St border is completed.

Next row (RS): Knit 7, place marker on needle, k 25 (27, 29) sts.

Following row: Purl to marker, slip marker, knit 7. This establishes position of front border.

Work to correspond to left front, reversing all shaping.

THIS PROJECT WAS KNIT WITH 34 (38, 42) balls of Muenchs GGH *Velour*, 100% polyamide nylon yarn, medium weight, 1oz/25g = approx 63yd/58m per ball, color #01.

SLEEVES

Make 2.

With yarn held double, cast on 34 (35, 36) sts.

Work in Garter St for 2"/5cm.

Work in Stockinette St, increasing 1 st each side every 8 (7, 7) rows 10 (11, 12) times. Work even on 54 (57, 60) sts until sleeve measures 19 (19 1/2, 20)"/48 (49.5, 51)cm.

Bind off all sts.

FINISHING

Sew shoulder seams. Mark side edges of fronts and back 9 (9½, 10)"/23 (24, 25.5)cm below shoulder seams for armholes. Sew top edge of a sleeve between markers on each side. Seam underarm and side edges.

Collar

With RS of work facing you, pick up and knit 14 (15, 16) sts along right front neck, 20 sts across back, 14 (15, 16) sts along left front neck. Work these 48 (50, 52) sts in Garter St for 5"/13cm. Bind off all sts.

> ## Design Tip
> This design would work very well in a soft merino, cashmere, or a wool and angora blend for a dressier look.

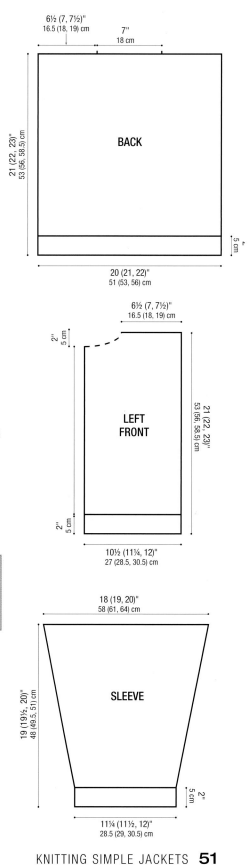

6½ (7, 7½)"
16.5 (18, 19) cm

7"
18 cm

21 (22, 23)"
53 (56, 58.5) cm

BACK

5 cm

20 (21, 22)"
51 (53, 56) cm

6½ (7, 7½)"
16.5 (18, 19) cm

2"
5 cm

21 (22, 23)"
53 (56, 58.5) cm

LEFT FRONT

2"
5 cm

10½ (11¼, 12)"
27 (28.5, 30.5) cm

18 (19, 20)"
58 (61, 64) cm

19 (19½, 20)"
48 (49.5, 51) cm

SLEEVE

2"
5 cm

11¼ (11½, 12)"
28.5 (29, 30.5) cm

the sequins

You can knit this shimmering evening jacket

in a very short time using #8 needles and an

extremely fine, sequin-embellished, kid

mohair. The stitch is simple stockinette, and

the only shaping is at the "V" in the front.

Experience Level
Easy

Sizes
Small, Medium/Large, X-Large

Finished Bust Measurements
35 (39, 41)"/89 (99, 104)cm Close Fit

Materials
Approx total: 650 (800, 1000)yd/594
(732, 914)m of kid mohair with
sequins fine-weight yarn

Knitting needles: 5mm (size 8 U.S.) *or
size to obtain gauge*

Double-pointed needles: 5mm (size 8
U.S.) for I-cord

Crochet hook: 5mm (size H/8)

Tapestry needle for sewing seams

Gauge
17 sts and 20 rows = 4"/10cm in
Stockinette Stitch

Always take time to check your gauge.

Pattern Stitches

Stockinette Stitch

Row 1 and all RS rows: Knit all stitches.

Row 2 and all WS rows: Purl all stitches.

Repeat rows 1 and 2 for pattern.

Garter Stitch

Knit every row.

Instructions

BACK

With regular straight needles, cast on 74 (78, 84) sts.

Work in Garter Stitch for 3 rows.

Now work in Stockinette Stitch until piece measures 19 (20, 21)"/48.5 (51, 53.5)cm from beginning.

Bind off all sts for shoulders and neck.

LEFT FRONT

Cast on 38 (44, 46) sts.

Work in Garter Stitch for 3 rows.

Work in Stockinette St until piece measures 10 (10½, 11)"/25.5 (27, 28)cm from beginning.

V-neck shaping

At front edge, decrease 1 st every 3 rows 10 (4, 6) times, then at same edge, every other row 6 (17, 15) times.

Work even on remaining 22 (23, 25) sts until piece measures same as back to shoulders.

Bind off all sts.

RIGHT FRONT

Work to correspond to left front, reversing shaping.

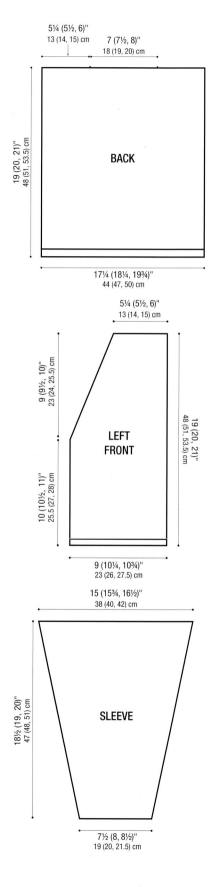

SLEEVES

Make 2.

Cast on 32 (34, 36) sts.

Work in Stockinette St, increasing 1 st each side every 5 rows 16 (16, 17) times.

Work even on 64 (66, 70) sts until sleeve measures 18½ (19, 20)"/ 47 (48.5, 51)cm from beginning.

Bind off all sts.

I-CORD TIES

Make 2.

With 2 double-pointed needles, cast on 3 sts.

Knit these 3 sts, * then slide sts to opposite end of needle and exchange needles so sts are on left needle with knit side of work facing you. Bringing yarn across the back of sts, knit them again; repeat from *, forming round cord, until cord measures 12"/30.5cm from beginning. Knit 3 together and fasten off.

FINISHING

Sew shoulder seams. Mark side edges of fronts and back 7½ (7¾, 8¼)"/19 (19.5, 21)cm below shoulder seams for armholes. Sew top edge of a sleeve to each side between markers. Sew underarm and side seams.

Crocheted edging

With right side of work facing you, start on bottom at right seam to crochet a row of single crochet (sc) all around outer edge of jacket, spacing sts to keep edges flat and smooth. When you have worked around to the beginning, turn work to crochet slip stitches around edge. Repeat on each sleeve edge.

Attach a tie securely to each front at the base of the V-neck.

THIS PROJECT WAS KNIT WITH 13 (16, 20) balls of Karabella *Sequins*, 100% super kid mohair yarn threaded with sequins, fine weight, approx 50yd/46m per ball, color copper/orange.

elegant kimono

Three rectangles and two squares combine to make a one-size-fits-all kimono-style jacket. Each piece is knit in stockinette from side to side using a cotton/linen yarn to create a softly draped, sophisticated look. The border is finished in single crochet to accent the simplicity of the kimono style.

Experience Level
Easy

Size
One size fits all.

Finished Measurements
44"/112cm across.

Materials
Approx total: 1853yd/1694m of cotton and linen blend lightweight yarn

Knitting needles: 4.5mm (size 7 U.S.) *or size to obtain gauge*

Crochet hook: 3.25 mm (size D/3)

Tapestry needle for sewing seams

Gauge
18 sts and 26 rows = 4"/10cm in Stockinette Stitch

Always take time to check your gauge.

Pattern Stitch

Stockinette Stitch

Row 1 and all RS rows: Knit all stitches.

Row 2 and all WS rows: Purl all stitches.

Repeat rows 1 and 2 for pattern.

Instructions

BACK

Piece is worked from side to side.

Cast on 86 sts.

Work in Stockinette Stitch until piece measure 44"/112cm from beginning.

Bind off all sts.

LEFT FRONT

Piece is worked side to side.

Cast on 86 sts.

Work in Stockinette St until piece measures 19"/48cm from beginning.

Bind off all sts.

RIGHT FRONT

Work same as for left front.

SLEEVES

Make 2.

Each sleeve is worked side to side.

Cast on 36 sts.

THIS PROJECT WAS KNIT WITH 17 balls of Muench GGH *Linova*, 74% cotton/26% linen yarn, lightweight, 1 3/4oz/50g = approx 109yd/100m per ball, color #002.

Work in Stockinette St until piece measures 18"/45.5cm from beginning.

Bind off all sts.

FINISHING

Sew shoulder seams. Mark side edges of fronts and back 9"/23cm below shoulder seams for sleeve placement. Sew long edge of a sleeve to each side between markers. Sew underarm and side seams.

Crocheted edging

With crochet hook and right side of work facing you, start on bottom edge at right seam to work a row of single crochet (sc) all around outer edges of jacket body, spacing sts to keep edges flat and smooth. When row is completed, turn work and sc for 6 more rows. Fasten off. Crochet around each sleeve edge in same manner.

Block lightly for a professional finish.

Design Tip

If sleeves edges are a bit too long, turn up crocheted cuff edge and tack in place.

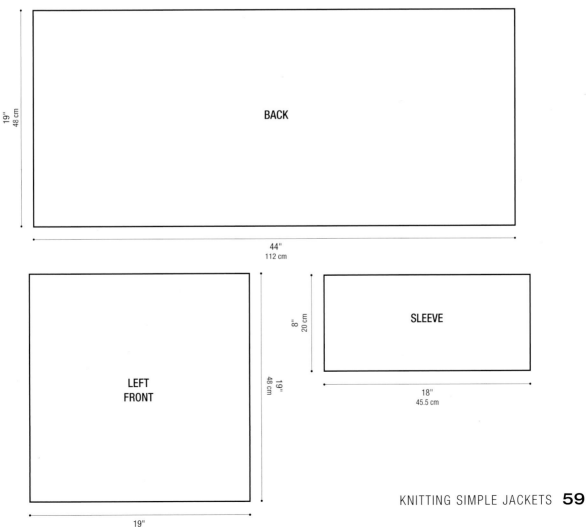

BACK

19"
48 cm

44"
112 cm

LEFT
FRONT

19"
48 cm

19"
48 cm

8"
20 cm

SLEEVE

18"
45.5 cm

vintage fur

Faux fur is so in vogue. Lightweight yet warm, with a collar that can be worn up or down, it's the perfect cold-weather jacket. Every woman needs a fur coat like this one.

Pattern Stitches

Stockinette Stitch
Row 1 and all RS rows: Knit all stitches.

Row 2 and all WS rows: Purl all stitches.

Repeat rows 1 and 2 for pattern.

Garter Stitch
Knit every row.

Instructions

BACK
Cast on 66 (68, 70, 74) sts.

Work in Garter Stitch for 3 rows.

Work in Stockinette Stitch until piece measures 26 (26, 27, 27¾)"/ 66 (66, 68.5, 70.5)cm from beginning.

Experience Level
Very Easy

Sizes
Small, Medium, Large, X-Large

Finished Bust Measurements
41 (43, 45, 47)"/104 (109, 114, 119.5)cm
Standard Fit

Materials
Approx total: 1235 (1330, 1520, 1615)yd/1129 (1216, 1390, 1477)m polyester and nylon bulky-weight yarn

Knitting needles: 5.5mm (size 9 U.S.) *or size to obtain gauge*

Crochet hook: 6.5mm (size K/10)

Tapestry needle for sewing seams

Gauge
13 sts and 20 rows = 4"/10cm in Stockinette Stitch

Always take time to check your gauge.

Shoulder shaping and collar

Bind off 21 (22, 23, 25) sts at the beginning of the next 2 rows.

Work on remaining 24 sts in Garter St for 4½"/11.5cm for collar.

Bind off all sts.

LEFT FRONT

Cast on 34 (36, 38, 40) sts.

Work in Garter St for 3 rows.

Work even in Stockinette St until piece measures same as back to shoulder shaping.

Shoulder shaping and collar

At arm edge, bind off 21 (23, 25, 27) sts.

Work on remaining 13 sts in Garter St for 4½"/11.5cm for collar.

Bind off all sts.

RIGHT FRONT

Work to correspond to left front, reversing shaping.

SLEEVES

Make 2.

Cast on 32 (32, 34, 36) sts.

Work in Garter St for 3 rows.

THIS PROJECT WAS KNIT WITH 13 (14, 16, 17) balls of Trendsetter Yarns *Vintage*, 60% polyester, 40% tactel nylon yarn, bulky weight, 1¾oz/50g = approx 95 yd/87m per ball, color #811.

Work in Stockinette St and increase 1 st each side every 8 (7, 7, 8) rows 13 (14, 14, 13) times.

Work even on 58 (60, 62, 62) sts until sleeve measures 21 (21, 22, 22½)"/53.5 (53.5, 56, 57)cm.

Bind off all sts.

FINISHING

Sew shoulder seams, easing edges to fit, then continue the seam up adjoining collar edges. Mark side edges of fronts and back 9 (9¼, 9 1/2, 9½)"/23 (23.5, 24, 24)cm for armholes. Sew top of a sleeve edge to each side between markers. Sew underarm and side seams.

Crocheted edging and button loops

Mark right front edge 16"/40.5cm up from bottom edge. With crochet hook, work a row of slip stitch around front edges and collar, making a 6-chain button loop at right front marker. Sew a purchased or crocheted button (see below) to left front opposite button loop.

Crocheted button

With crochet hook, chain 5 and join with slip stitch in first chain to form a ring.

Round 1: Work 7 single crochet (sc) in ring. Do not join sts, but work around and around. Mark beginning of each round.

Round 2: Work 2 sc in each sc around.

Round 3: Work sc in each sc around. Cut yarn leaving a long end. Using tapestry needle, draw yarn through top of each st on last round and draw them tightly together. Leave button unstuffed and securely fasten off.

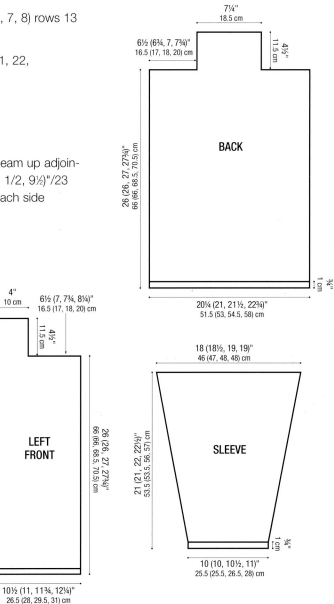

With chunky, soft, merino wool, big needles, and the simple garter stitch, you can knit this hooded winter coat in no time. The shoulders are dropped, the sleeves deeply cuffed, the hood generous and cozy, and the length is almost to the knee.

hooded
big coat

Experience Level
Very Easy

Sizes
Small, Medium/Large, X-Large

Finished Bust Measurements
37 (41½, 46)"/94 (105.5, 117)cm
Standard Fit

Materials
Approx total: 1566 (1740,
2001)yd/1432 (1591, 1830)m of
wool bulky-weight yarn

Knitting needles: 9mm (size 13 U.S.) for
jacket *or size to obtain gauge*

Circular needle: 29"/74cm, 9mm (size
13 U.S.) for belt

Tapestry needle for sewing seams

Gauge
10 sts and 20 rows = 4"/10cm in
Garter Stitch; 20 rows = 10 ridges

Always take time to check your gauge.

Pattern Stitch
Garter Stitch
Knit every row.

Instructions

BACK
With straight needles, cast on 45 (50, 55) sts.

Work in Garter Stitch until piece measures 28 (29, 30)"/71(73.5, 76)cm from beginning.

Bind off all sts for shoulders and neck.

LEFT FRONT
With straight needles, cast on 24 (27, 30) sts.

Work in Garter St until piece measures 26½ (27 1/2, 28½)"/67(69.5, 72)cm from beginning.

Neck shaping
At front edge, bind off 3 (4, 5) sts once, then at same edge bind off 4 sts every other row twice.

Work even on 13 (15, 17) sts until piece measures same as back to shoulders.

Bind off all sts.

RIGHT FRONT
Work to correspond to left front, reversing shaping.

SLEEVES

Make 2.

With straight needles, cast on 38 (40, 42) sts.

Work in Garter St until sleeve measures 20 (21, 22)"/51 (53.5, 56)cm from beginning.

Bind off all sts.

BELT

With circular needle, cast on 140 sts.

Work in Garter St for 15 rows.

Bind off all sts.

FINISHING

Sew shoulder seams. Mark side edges of fronts and back 7¾ (8, 8½)"/19.5 (20, 21.5)cm below shoulder seams for armholes. Sew top edge of a sleeve to each side between markers. Sew underarm and side seams.

Hood

With right side of work facing you, pick up and knit 15 sts along right front neck edge, 18 (20, 22) sts across back neck, and 15 sts along left front neck edge for a total of 48 (50, 52) sts.

Work in Garter St for 11"/28cm from beginning at neck edge. Form center top split as follows:

On next row, knit 24 (25, 26) sts, attach a new ball of yarn and with new yarn, knit to end.

Working each side with its own yarn, continue in Garter St and decrease 1 st along each edge of split every other row until hood measures 16"/40.5cm from neck edge.

Bind off all sts on each side.

Matching split and bound-off edges of one side to those of other side, sew center top seam of hood.

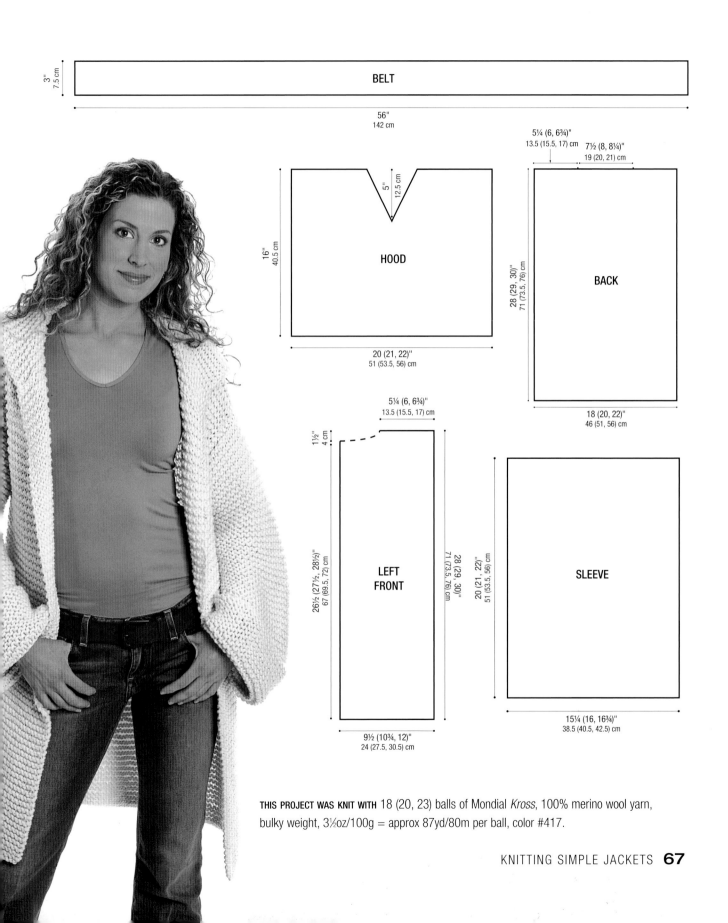

BELT

3"
7.5 cm

56"
142 cm

HOOD

5"
12.5 cm

16"
40.5 cm

20 (21, 22)"
51 (53.5, 56) cm

BACK

5¼ (6, 6¾)"
13.5 (15.5, 17) cm

7½ (8, 8¼)"
19 (20, 21) cm

28 (29, 30)"
71 (73.5, 76) cm

18 (20, 22)"
46 (51, 56) cm

LEFT FRONT

5¼ (6, 6¾)"
13.5 (15.5, 17) cm

1½"
4 cm

26½ (27½, 28½)"
67 (69.5, 72) cm

28 (29, 30)"
71 (73.5, 76) cm

9½ (10¾, 12)"
24 (27.5, 30.5) cm

SLEEVE

20 (21, 22)"
51 (53.5, 56) cm

15¼ (16, 16¾)"
38.5 (40.5, 42.5) cm

THIS PROJECT WAS KNIT WITH 18 (20, 23) balls of Mondial *Kross*, 100% merino wool yarn, bulky weight, 3½oz/100g = approx 87yd/80m per ball, color #417.

A simple interpretation of the
Chanel style is knitted in a
silky, summery, and bold
lightweight cotton. The trim
is a double strand of satiny
ribbon in a contrasting color
and serves to define and
emphasize the timeless
design. Around the waist is a
narrow cord of crocheted
double-strand ribbon.

cotton chanel

Experience Level
Easy

Sizes
Small, Medium/Large, X-Large

Finished Bust Measurements
39 (41, 43)"/99 (104, 109)cm
   Standard Fit

Materials
Approx total: Main color (MC): 1230
   (1435, 1640)yd/1125 (1312, 1500)m
   of mercerized cotton lightweight yarn

Contrasting color (CC): 284yd/260m of
   polyamide/nylon ribbon-type lightweight yarn

Knitting needles: 3.75mm (size 5 U.S.)
   or size to obtain gauge

Crochet hook: 3.75mm (size F/5)

Tapestry needle for sewing seams

Gauge
20 sts and 28 rows = 4"/10cm in
   Stockinette Stitch

Always take time to check your gauge.

Pattern Stitch
Stockinette Stitch
Row 1 and all RS rows: Knit all stitches.

Row 2 and all WS rows: Purl all stitches.

Repeat rows 1 and 2 for pattern.

Instructions

BACK
With main color (MC), cast on 95 (100, 105) sts.

Work in Stockinette Stitch until piece measures 24 (25, 26)"/61(63.5, 66)cm from beginning.

Bind off all sts for shoulders and neck.

LEFT FRONT
With MC, cast on 50 (53, 55) sts.

Work in Stockinette St until piece measures 22 (23, 24)"/56 (58.5, 61)cm from beginning.

Shape neck
At front edge, bind off 8 (10, 11) sts once, then at same edge, bind off 3 sts every other row once, then 2 sts every other row 5 times.

Work even, if needed, on 29 (30, 31) sts until piece measures same as back to shoulder.

Bind off all sts.

RIGHT FRONT
Work to correspond to left front, reversing shaping.

SLEEVES

Make 2.

With MC, cast on 56 (58, 60) sts.

Work in Stockinette St, increasing 1 st each side every 11 (10, 9) rows 12 (13, 15) times.

Work even on 80 (84, 90) sts until sleeve measures 19 (19½, 20)"/48 (49.5, 51)cm from beginning.

Bind off all sts.

TIE BELT

With crochet hook and 2 strands on contrasting color (CC) held together, crochet a chain 72"/183cm long.

Row 1: Work a single crochet (sc) in second ch from hook, sc in each remaining ch to end. Fasten off.

FINISHING

Sew shoulder seams. Mark side edge of front and back 8 (8½, 9)"/20 (21.5, 23)cm below shoulder seams for armholes. Sew top edge of a sleeve to each side between markers. Sew underarm and side seams.

Crocheted edges

With right side of work facing you, using crochet hook and 2 strands of CC held together, start on bottom edge at right seam to crochet a row of single crochet (sc) all around outer edges of jacket body, spacing sts to keep edges flat and smooth. When you have worked around to starting point, work a row of reverse sc (see below) over sts just made. Repeat sc and reverse sc rows around each sleeve edge.

Reverse sc

A reverse sc is a single crochet st worked backwards from left to right (instead of right to left) as follows:

With right side of work facing you, insert hook from front to back into next st to the right, yarn over and draw the yarn through the st, then yarn over again and draw yarn through both loops on hook to complete the reverse sc.

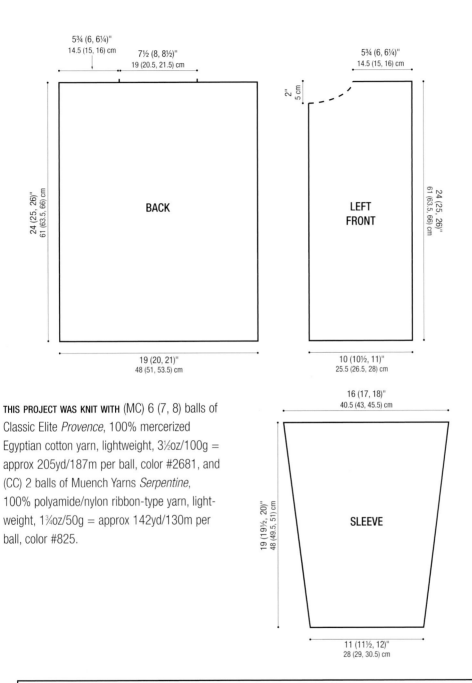

5¾ (6, 6¼)"
14.5 (15, 16) cm

7½ (8, 8½)"
19 (20.5, 21.5) cm

BACK

24 (25, 26)"
61 (63.5, 66) cm

19 (20, 21)"
48 (51, 53.5) cm

5¾ (6, 6¼)"
14.5 (15, 16) cm

2"
5 cm

LEFT FRONT

24 (25, 26)"
61 (63.5, 66) cm

10 (10½, 11)"
25.5 (26.5, 28) cm

THIS PROJECT WAS KNIT WITH (MC) 6 (7, 8) balls of Classic Elite *Provence*, 100% mercerized Egyptian cotton yarn, lightweight, 3½oz/100g = approx 205yd/187m per ball, color #2681, and (CC) 2 balls of Muench Yarns *Serpentine*, 100% polyamide/nylon ribbon-type yarn, lightweight, 1¾oz/50g = approx 142yd/130m per ball, color #825.

16 (17, 18)"
40.5 (43, 45.5) cm

SLEEVE

19 (19½, 20)"
48 (49.5, 51) cm

11 (11½, 12)"
28 (29, 30.5) cm

TIE BELT

72"
183 cm

asymmetrical poncho

Worn smartly off to one side, this poncho will garner many double-takes. Knit in one piece on large needles, it's essentially a rectangle with neck shaping.

Experience Level
Very Easy

Size
One size fits all.

Finished Measurements
30" x 22½"/76 x 57cm

Materials
Approx total: 520yd/475m of wool, nylon, and acrylic blend bulky-weight yarn

Knitting needles: 5.5mm (size 9 U.S.) *or size to obtain gauge*

Crochet hook: 6mm (size J/10)

Tapestry needle for sewing seams

Gauge
11 sts and 18 rows = 4"/10cm in Stockinette Stitch

Always take time to check your gauge.

Pattern Stitch

Stockinette Stitch

Row 1 and all RS rows: Knit all stitches.

Row 2 and all WS rows: Purl all stitches.

Repeat rows 1 and 2 for pattern.

Instructions

PONCHO

Cast on 62 sts.

Work in Stockinette Stitch until piece measures 17"/43cm from beginning, ending with a purl row.

Neck opening

With right side of work facing you, decrease 1 st at right-hand edge (beginning of knit rows) every other row until piece measures 30"/76cm from beginning. Piece should now be about 12"/30.5cm wide with about 33 sts left on needle.

Continue in Stockinette St and increase 1 st at same edge every other row until you again have 62 sts on needle.

Work even until piece measures 60"/152.5cm from beginning. Both sections should measure the same length from the narrowest row.

FINISHING

Fold poncho in half along narrow row at center, with wrong sides together and right sides facing out. Leaving bottom and long straight edge open, seam shaped edge as follows: Leaving bottom 11"/28cm open, sew the remaining 6"/15cm seam up to the start of the neck opening.

Crocheted edging

With crochet hook, work a row of single crochet (sc) around neck edge, spacing sts to keep edge flat and smooth.

THIS PROJECT WAS KNIT WITH 8 balls of Muench GGH *Capella*, 40% wool/30% nylon/30% acrylic yarn, bulky weight, 1¾oz/50g = approx 65yd/59m per ball, color #1.

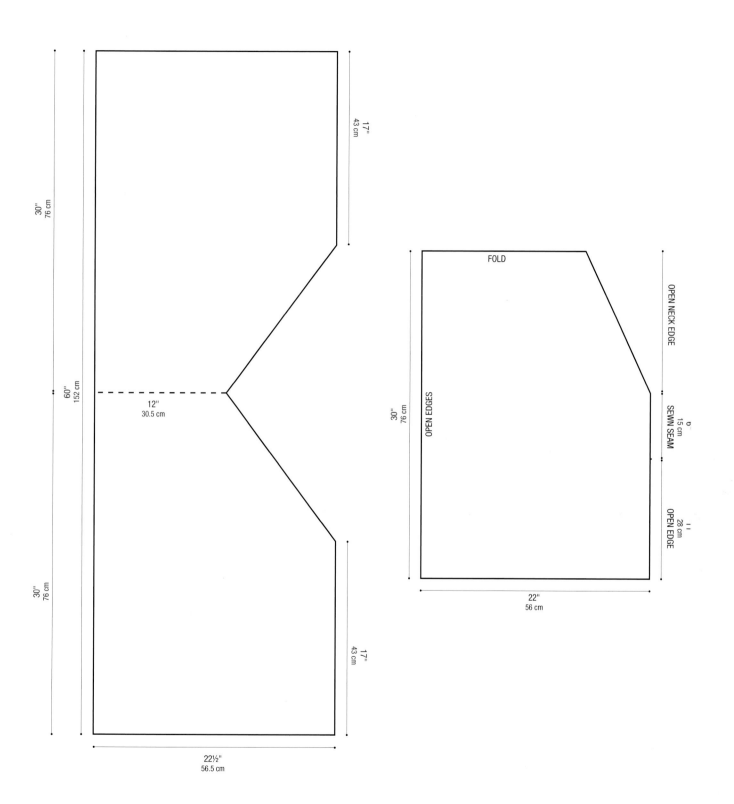

30"
76 cm

17"
43 cm

60"
152 cm

12"
30.5 cm

30"
76 cm

17"
43 cm

22½"
56.5 cm

FOLD

OPEN NECK EDGE

OPEN EDGES

6"
15 cm
SEWN SEAM

11"
28 cm
OPEN EDGE

30"
76 cm

22"
56 cm

A strand of pashmina and one of silk are held and knit together into a chic cardigan coat, complete with deep cuffs, a self-belt, and a doubled funnel-neck collar.

pashmina
and silk

Pattern Stitch
Rib Stitch
(multiple of 5 sts)

Row 1 (right side): *Knit 3, purl 2; repeat from * across.

Row 2: *Knit 2, purl 3; repeat from * across.

Repeat rows 1 and 2 for pattern.

Instructions

BACK
With one strand of each yarn held together, cast on 140 sts.

Work in Rib Stitch pattern until piece measures 30"/76cm from beginning.

Bind off all sts for shoulders and neck.

LEFT FRONT
With 1 strand of each yarn held together, cast on 75 sts.

Work in pattern until piece measures 27½"/70cm from beginning.

Neck shaping
At front neck edge, keeping continuity of pattern as established, bind off 5 sts once, then 4 sts every other row 6 times.

Bind off remaining 46 sts for shoulder.

RIGHT FRONT
Work to correspond to left front, reversing shaping.

SLEEVES

Make 2.

With 1 strand of each yarn held together, cast on 75 sts.

Work in pattern and, keeping continuity of pattern, increase 1 st each side every 5 rows 21 times, working added sts in pattern.

Work even on 117 sts until sleeve measures 20"/51cm from beginning.

Bind off all sts.

BELT

With 1 strand of each yarn held together, cast on 25 sts.

Work in pattern until piece measures 56"/142cm from beginning.

Bind off all sts.

FINISHING

Sew shoulder seams. Mark side edges of fronts and back 9"/23cm below shoulder seams for armholes. Sew top edge of a sleeve to each side between markers. Sew underarm and side seams.

THIS PROJECT WAS KNIT WITH 2 cones of Joseph Galler *Jasmine*, 100% silk yarn, lightweight, 1 pound/455g = approx 1250yd/1140m per cone, color #7005, and 11 balls of Joseph Galler *Pashmina*, 100% pashmina cashmere yarn, fine weight, 1¾oz/50g = approx 170yd/155m per ball, color Bordeaux.

Collar

With right side of work facing you, pick up and knit 83 sts evenly spaced around neck edge and work as follows:

Row 1 (wrong side): Purl 3, *knit 2, purl 3; repeat from * across.

Row 2: Knit 3, *purl 2, knit 3; repeat from * across.

Repeat these 2 rows for pattern until collar measures 7"/18cm from neck edge.

Bind off all sts loosely in pattern.

Fold top half of collar to inside and sew bound-off edge to base of collar. Sew layers together at each front edge of collar.

Design Tip
Sleeves are especially long so they can be turned up for a deep cuff. Cuff can be tacked to stay in place.

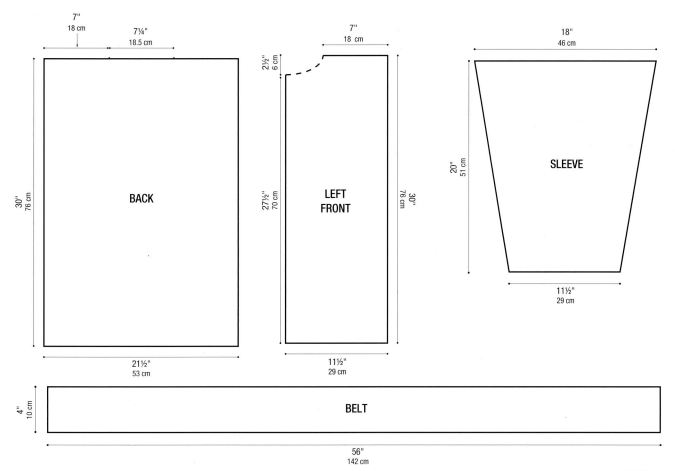

Here's a favorite stitch that looks complicated but isn't. A four-row pattern with the first and third row in a basic purl stitch, it works well in an angora blend yarn. A circular needle is used to complete the rolled edges.

trinity stitch

Experience Level
Intermediate

Sizes
Small, Medium/Large, X-Large

Finished Bust Measurements
39½ (42, 45)"/100 (107, 114)cm
  Standard Fit

Materials
Approx total: 1488 (1612,
  1736)yd/1361 (1474, 1587)m of
  angora and wool blend medium-
  weight yarn

Knitting needles: 5.5mm (size 9 U.S.) *or
  size to obtain gauge*

Circular needle: 29"/74cm or
  36"/91.5cm, 5.5mm (size 9 U.S.)

Tapestry needle for sewing seams

Gauge
18 sts and 16 rows = 4"/10cm in pattern stitch

Always take time to check your gauge.

Pattern Stitches

Trinity Stitch
(multiple of 4 sts plus 2)

Row 1 (right side): Purl all stitches.

Row 2: Knit 1, *work (knit 1, purl 1, knit 1) all in the next stitch, purl 3 together; repeat from * across to last st, knit 1.

Row 3: Purl all stitches.

Row 4: Knit 1, *purl 3 together, work (knit 1, purl 1, knit 1) all in the next stitch; repeat from * across to last st, knit 1.

Repeat rows 1 through 4 for pattern.

Stockinette Stitch
Row 1 and all RS rows: Knit all stitches.

Row 2 and all WS rows: Purl all stitches.

Repeat rows 1 and 2 for pattern.

Instructions

BACK
Cast on 86 (90, 94) sts.

Work in Trinity Stitch pattern until piece measures 21 (21½, 22)"/53 (54.5, 56)cm from beginning.

Bind off all sts for shoulders and neck.

LEFT FRONT
Cast on 46 (50, 54) sts.

Work in pattern until piece measures 16½"/42cm from beginning.

Neck shaping

At neck edge, bind off 3 (4, 5) sts once, then at same edge bind off 2 sts every other row 8 (9, 10) times, keeping continuity of pattern.

Work even, if needed, on 27 (28, 29) sts until piece measures same as back to shoulder.

Bind off all sts.

RIGHT FRONT

Work to correspond to left front, reversing shaping.

SLEEVES

Make 2.

Cast on 42 (46, 46) sts.

Work in pattern and, keeping continuity of pattern, increase 1 st each side every 4 rows 15 (15, 10) times, then every 3 rows 4 (4, 12) times more, working added sts in pattern.

Work even on 80 (84, 90) sts until sleeve measures 19 (19, 20)"/48.5 (48.5, 51)cm from beginning.

Bind off all sts.

THIS PROJECT WAS KNIT WITH 12 (13, 14) balls of Classic Elite *Lush*, 50% angora/50% wool yarn, medium weight, 1¾oz/50g = approx 124yd/113m per ball, color #4475.

FINISHING

Sew shoulder seams. Mark side edges of fronts and back 9 (9½, 10)"/23 (24, 25.5)cm below shoulder seams for armholes. Sew top edge of a sleeve to each side between markers. Sew underarm and side seams.

Knitted edging

With long circular needle and right side of work facing you, starting on bottom at right seam, pick up and knit stitches evenly all around outer edges of jacket body, spacing sts to keep edges flat and smooth. Join last st to first st and knit all sts for 8 rounds. Bind off all sts. Edges will curl forward as shown in photograph.

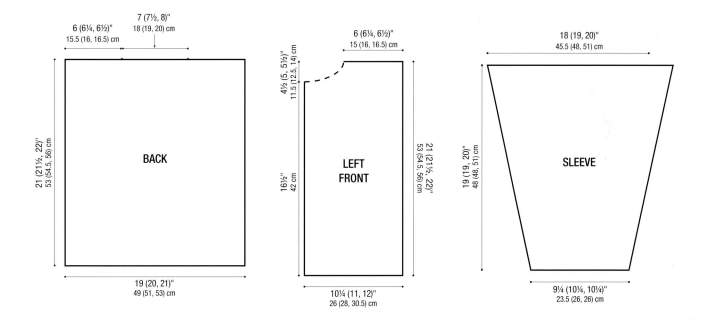

BACK

6 (6¼, 6½)"
15.5 (16, 16.5) cm

7 (7½, 8)"
18 (19, 20) cm

21 (21½, 22)"
53 (54.5, 56) cm

19 (20, 21)"
49 (51, 53) cm

LEFT FRONT

6 (6¼, 6½)"
15 (16, 16.5) cm

4½ (5, 5½)"
11.5 (12.5, 14) cm

16½"
42 cm

21 (21½, 22)"
53 (54.5, 56) cm

10¼ (11, 12)"
26 (28, 30.5) cm

SLEEVE

18 (19, 20)"
45.5 (48, 51) cm

19 (19, 20)"
48 (48, 51) cm

9¼ (10¼, 10¼)"
23.5 (26, 26) cm

This jacket showcases an eight-row cable pattern, which is very easy to master. A smooth cashmere and silk yarn shows off the subtle pattern. The edges are picked up on a circular needle, knit for a few rows, and allowed to roll naturally for an unusual border.

shadow
cable jacket

Experience Level
Intermediate

Sizes
Small, Medium/Large, X-Large

Finished Bust Measurements
36 (42, 46)"/91 (106, 117)cm
　Standard Fit

Materials
Approx total: 1375 (1500,
　1625)yd/1257 (1372, 1486)m of
　cashmere and silk blend medium-
　weight yarn

Knitting needles: 5mm (size 8 U.S.) *or
　size to obtain gauge*

Circular needle: 29"/74cm or
　36"/91.5cm, 5mm (size 8 U.S.)

Circular needle, 16"/40.5cm, 5mm (size
　8 U.S.)

Cable needle

Tapestry needle for sewing seams

Gauge
22 sts and 28 rows = 4"/10cm in pat-
　tern stitch

Always take time to check your gauge.

Pattern Stitch
Shadow Cable
(multiple of 8 sts plus 2)

Row 1 (wrong side): Purl all stitches.

Row 2: Knit all stitches.

Row 3: Purl all stitches.

Row 4: Knit 1, *slip next 2 sts to cable needle and hold in back of work, knit next 2 sts from left needle, knit 2 sts from cable needle, knit 4; repeat from * across to last st, knit 1.

Row 5: Purl all stitches.

Row 6: Knit all stitches.

Row 7: Purl all stitches.

Row 8: Knit 1, *knit 4, slip next 2 sts to cable needle and hold in front of work, knit next 2 sts from left needle, knit 2 sts from cable needle; repeat from * across to last st, knit 1.

Repeat rows 1 through 8 for pattern.

Instructions

BACK
With straight needles, cast on 98 (114, 122) sts.

Work in Shadow Cable pattern until piece measures 11½ (12½, 13)"/29 (32, 33)cm from beginning.

Armhole shaping

Bind off 8 sts at beginning of next 2 rows

Work even on 82 (98, 106) sts until piece measures 19 (21, 22)"/48.5 (53, 56)cm from beginning.

Bind off all sts for shoulders and neck.

LEFT FRONT

With straight needles, cast on 50 (58, 66) sts

Work in pattern until piece measures same as back to armholes.

Armhole shaping

At arm edge, bind off 8 sts once.

Work even on 42 (50, 58) sts until piece measures 17 (19, 20)"/43 (48.5, 51)cm from beginning.

Neck shaping

At front edge, bind off 6 (8, 8) sts once, then at same edge, bind off 3 (3, 4) sts every other row 5 times.

Work even, if needed, on 21 (27, 30) sts until piece measures same as back to shoulders.

Bind off all sts.

RIGHT FRONT

Work to correspond to left front, reversing all shaping.

THIS PROJECT WAS KNIT WITH 11 (12, 13) balls of Classic Elite *Posh*, 30% cashmere, 70% silk yarn, medium weight, 1¾oz/50g = approx 125yd/114m per ball, color #93050.

SLEEVES

Make 2.

Cast on 58 (58, 66) sts.

Work in pattern and, keeping continuity of pattern as established, increase 1 st each side every 10 (7, 8) rows 12 (18, 17) times, working added sts in pattern.

Work even on 82 (94, 100) sts until piece measures 19½ (20½, 21)"/49.5 (52, 53)cm from beginning.

Bind off all sts.

FINISHING

Sew shoulder seams. Sew top edge of a sleeve to straight edge of each arm-hole; sew top side edge of sleeve to adjacent bound-off sts of armhole. Sew underarm and side seams.

Knitted edging

With long circular needle and right side of work facing you, start on bottom at right seam to pick up and knit sts all around outer edge of jacket, spacing sts to keep edges smooth and flat. Knit in rounds for 7 rounds. Bind off all sts. Edges will curl forward as shown in photograph.

With short circular needle (see note below), knit a 7-round edging around each sleeve edge in same manner.

Note: If it is more comfortable, use a set of same-sized double-pointed needles, instead of circular needle, to keep sleeve sts from stretching too much as you work.

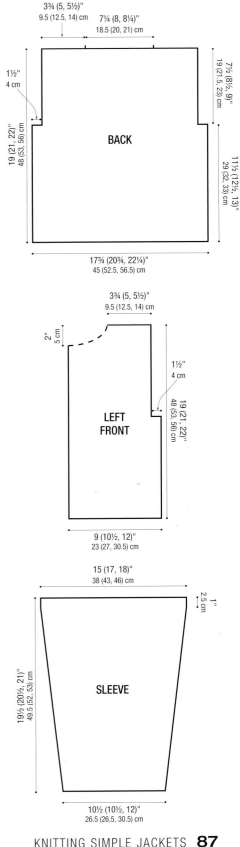

BACK

3¾ (5, 5½)"
9.5 (12.5, 14) cm

7¼ (8, 8¼)"
18.5 (20, 21) cm

1½"
4 cm

7½ (8½, 9)"
19 (21.5, 23) cm

19 (21, 22)"
48 (53, 56) cm

11½ (12½, 13)"
29 (32, 33) cm

17¾ (20¾, 22¼)"
45 (52.5, 56.5) cm

LEFT FRONT

3¾ (5, 5½)"
9.5 (12.5, 14) cm

2"
5 cm

1½"
4 cm

19 (21, 22)"
48 (53, 56) cm

9 (10½, 12)"
23 (27, 30.5) cm

SLEEVE

15 (17, 18)"
38 (43, 46) cm

1"
2.5 cm

19½ (20½, 21)"
49.5 (52, 53) cm

10½ (10½, 12)"
26.5 (26.5, 30.5) cm

Here's an easy-to-knit garter stitch project in the color of sunshine. There are four crocheted loops for purchased buttons, and a sporty hood. If you would like a collar instead of a hood, the instructions are included.

sleeveless jacket

Experience Level
Easy

Sizes
Small, Medium/Large, X-Large

Finished Bust Measurements
41 (45, 49)"/104 (114.5, 124.5)cm
  Standard Fit

Materials
Approx total: 783 (870, 957)yd/716
  (796, 875)m of polyamide nylon
  medium-weight yarn

Knitting needles: 6mm (size 10 U.S.) *or
  size to obtain gauge*

Crochet hook: 5mm (size H/8)

Four buttons

Gauge
12 sts and 20 rows = 4"/10cm

Always take time to check your gauge.

Pattern Stitch
Garter Stitch
Knit every row.

Instructions

BACK
Cast on 60 (66, 72) sts.

Work in Garter Stitch until piece measures 13 (13½, 14)"/33 (34, 35.5)cm from beginning.

Armhole shaping
Bind off 3 sts at beginning of next 2 rows.

Work even on 54 (60, 66) sts until piece measures 22 (23, 24)"/56 (58.5, 61)cm from beginning.

Bind off all sts for shoulders and neck.

LEFT FRONT
Cast on 32 (35, 38) sts.

Work in Garter St until piece measures same as back to armholes.

Armhole shaping
At arm edge, bind off 3 sts once.

Work even on 29 (32, 35) sts until piece measures 20½ (21½, 22½)"/52 (54.5, 57)cm from beginning.

Neck shaping

At front edge, bind off 5 sts every other row twice, then at same edge bind off 4 sts every other row once.

Work even, if needed, on 15 (18, 21) sts until piece measures same as back to shoulder.

Bind off all sts.

RIGHT FRONT

Work to correspond to left front, reversing shaping.

FINISHING

Sew shoulder and side seams. Work hood or collar, whichever you prefer, as follows:

Hood

With right side of work facing you, pick up and knit 18 sts along right front neck edge, 24 sts across back neck, 18 sts along left front neck edge for a total of 60 sts.

Work in Garter St until hood measures 11"/28cm from beginning at neck edge. Form center top split as follows:

On next row, knit 30 sts, attach a new ball of yarn and with new yarn, complete row. Work each side separately with its own yarn and decrease 1 st at

THIS PROJECT WAS KNIT WITH 9 (10, 11) balls of Muench GGH *Esprit*, 100% polyamide nylon yarn, medium weight, 1¾oz/50g = approx 87yd/80m per ball, color #17.

each edge of split every other row until hood measures 16"/40.5cm from beginning.

Bind off all sts on each side.

Matching split and bound-off edges of one side to those of opposite side, sew center top seam.

Collar

With right side of work facing you, pick up and knit 18 sts along right front neck edge, 24 sts across back neck, 18 sts along left front neck edge for a total of 60 sts.

Work in Garter St for 5"/12.5cm.

Bind off all sts.

Button loops

Mark right front edge for 4 evenly spaced button loops. For each loop, attach yarn at marker, and with crochet hook, make 6 chain sts, slip stitch in first st at base of chain-6 to form loop. Fasten off securely.

Sew buttons to left front, opposite loops.

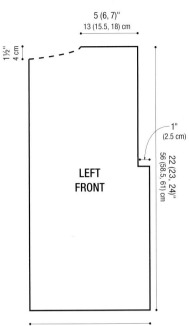

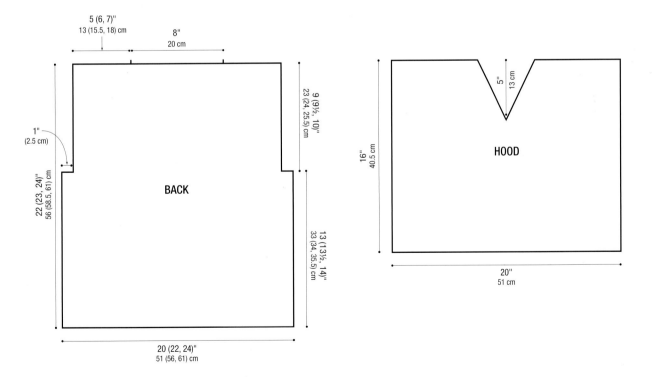

ribbon jacket

A fast-flowing slip stitch on very large

needles makes this jacket a breeze to knit,

and shows the ribbon off at its shiny best.

The style is flattering and easy to wear with

a self-belt that can also be used as a scarf.

Experience Level
Easy

Sizes
Small, Medium/Large, X-Large

Finished Bust Measurements
39 (41½, 45)"/99 (105.5, 114)cm
   Standard Fit

Materials
Approx total: 1200 (1320, 1440)yd/1097
   (1207, 1317)m of polyamide bulky-
   weight yarn

Knitting needles: 10mm (size 15 U.S.)
   or size to obtain gauge

Crochet hook: 6mm (size J/10)

Tapestry needle for sewing seams

Gauge
13 sts and 22 rows = 4"/10cm in
   pattern

Always take time to check your gauge.

Pattern Stitch

Slip Stitch Pattern

(multiple of 3 sts plus 1)

Row 1 (RS): *Knit 1, with yarn in front slip 2 sts purlwise*; repeat from * to *, end knit 1.

Row 2: Purl all sts.

Repeat rows 1 and 2 for pattern.

Instructions

BACK

Cast on 64 (67, 73) sts.

Work in Slip Stitch pattern until piece measures 20 (20, 21)"/51 (51, 53.5)cm from beginning.

Bind off all sts for shoulders and neck.

LEFT FRONT

Cast on 31 (34, 37) sts.

Work in pattern until piece measures 18 (18, 19)"/45.5 (45.5, 48)cm from beginning.

Neck shaping

At front edge, bind off 2 (2, 3) sts once, then 2 sts every other row 4 (5, 5) times.

Work even, if needed, on remaining 21 (22, 24) sts until piece measures same as back to shoulder.

Bind off all sts.

RIGHT FRONT

Work to correspond to left front, reversing shaping.

SLEEVES

Make 2.

Cast on 31 (31, 34) sts.

Work in pattern and, keeping continuity of pattern as established, increase 1 st each side every 7 rows 12 (14, 14) times.

Work even on 55 (59, 62) sts until sleeve measures 19 (19, 20)"/48 (48, 51)cm from beginning.

Bind off all sts.

FINISHING

Sew shoulder seams. Mark side edges of fronts and back 8½ (9, 9½)"/21.5 (23, 24)cm below shoulder seams for armholes. Sew top edge of a sleeve on each side between markers. Sew underarm and side seams.

Crocheted edging

With crochet hook, work a row of slip stitches all around outer edge of jacket, spacing sts to keep edges flat and smooth. Repeat around each sleeve edge.

THIS PROJECT WAS KNIT WITH 10 (11, 12) balls of Trendsetter *Segue*, 100% polyamide yarn, bulky weight, 3½oz/100g = approx 120yd/110m per ball, color #100.

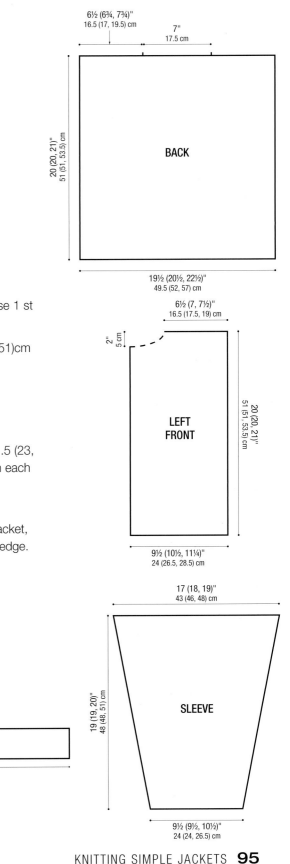

mohair hoodie

Don't be surprised when you find yourself reaching for this hoodie time and time again to go with everything from jeans to skirts. Using large needles, it's simple to knit the body in stockinette, with ribbing at the cuffs and bottom.

Experience Level
Easy

Sizes
Small, Medium/Large, X-Large

Finished Bust Measurements
42 (44, 47)"/106.5 (112, 119.5)cm
  Standard Fit

Materials
Approx total: 810 (900, 990)yd/741 (823, 905)m of mohair, wool, and nylon blend medium-weight yarn

Knitting needles: 6mm (size 10 U.S.) *or size to obtain gauge*

Crochet hook: 5mm (size H/8)

Tapestry needle for sewing seams

Gauge
12 sts and 16 rows = 4"/10cm in
  Stockinette Stitch

Always take time to check your gauge.

Pattern Stitches
Stockinette Stitch
Row 1 and all RS rows: Knit all stitches.

Row 2 and all WS rows: Purl all stitches.

Repeat rows 1 and 2 for pattern.

Rib Stitch #1
(multiple of 4 sts)

Row 1: *Knit 2, purl 2; repeat from * across.

Repeat row 1 for pattern.

Rib Stitch #2
(multiple of 4 sts plus 2)

Row 1: Knit 2, *purl 2, knit 2; repeat from * across.

Row 2: Purl 2, *knit 2, purl 2; repeat from * across.

Repeat rows 1 and 2 for pattern.

Instructions

BACK

Cast on 62 (64, 66) sts.

Work in Rib Stitch #2 (#1, #2) for 3"/7.5cm.

Work in Stockinette Stitch until piece measures 20 (21, 22)"/51 (53.5, 56)cm from beginning.

Bind off all sts for shoulders and neck.

LEFT FRONT

Cast on 32 (34, 38) sts.

Work in Rib St #1 (#2, #2) for 3"/7.5cm.

Work in Stockinette St until piece measures 17 (18, 19)"/43 (45.5, 48)cm from beginning.

Neck shaping

At front edge, bind off 3 (3, 5) sts once, then 4 sts every other row 3 times, then 2 sts every other row twice.

Work even on 13 (15, 17) sts, if needed, until piece measures same as back to shoulders.

Bind off all sts.

RIGHT FRONT

Work to correspond to left front, reversing shaping.

SLEEVES

Make 2.

Cast on 30 (32, 36) sts.

Work in Rib St #2 (#1, # 2) for 3"/7.5cm.

Work in Stockinette St, increasing 1 st each side every 5 rows 6 times, then every 5 (6, 6) rows 6 times.

Work even on 54 (56, 60 sts) until sleeve measures 19 (20, 21)"/48.5 (51, 53)cm from beginning.

Bind off all sts.

FINISHING

Sew shoulder seams.

Design Tip

Brush this mohair lightly with a hairbrush to soften and fluff it.

Hood

With right side of work facing you, pick up and knit 22 (23, 24) sts along right front neck edge, 24 (24, 26) sts across back neck, 22 (23, 24) sts along left front neck for a total of 68 (70, 74) sts.

Work in Stockinette St, decreasing 1 st each side every 10 rows and at the same time, when hood measures 9"/23cm from neck edge, form center split as follows:

Work halfway across next row, attach a new ball of ball and with new yarn complete row. Now work each side separately with its own yarn and continue to decrease at outer edges as before and decrease 1 st at each split edge every 6 rows 4 times.

When hood measures 16"/40.5cm, bind off all remaining sts on each side.

Matching split and bound-off edge on one side to those on opposite side, sew center top seam of hood.

Mark side edges of fronts and back 9 (9½, 10)"/23 (24, 25.5)cm below shoulder seams for armholes. Sew top edge of a sleeve to each side between markers. Sew underarm and side seams.

Crocheted button loops

Mark placement for 4 button loops on right front edge, with the first about 1"/2.5cm above bottom edge, the last at neck edge, and the rest evenly spaced between.

For each button loop, attach yarn at marker, chain 6, slip stitch at base of chain and securely fasten off.

Sew on purchased or crocheted buttons (see below) to left front opposite button loops.

Crocheted button

With crochet hook, chain 5 and join with slip stitch in first chain to form a ring.

Round 1: Work 7 single crochet (sc) in ring. Do not join, but work around and around. Mark beginning of each round.

Round 2: Work 2 sc in each sc around.

Round 3: Work 1 sc in each sc around. Cut yarn, leaving a long end. Using tapestry needle, draw yarn through top of each st on last round and draw them tightly together. Leave button unstuffed and securely fasten off.

THIS PROJECT WAS KNIT WITH 9 (10, 11) balls of Classic Elite La Gran, 76.5% mohair/17.5% wool/6% nylon yarn, medium weight, 1 1/2 oz/42g = approx 90yd/82m per ball, color #6589.

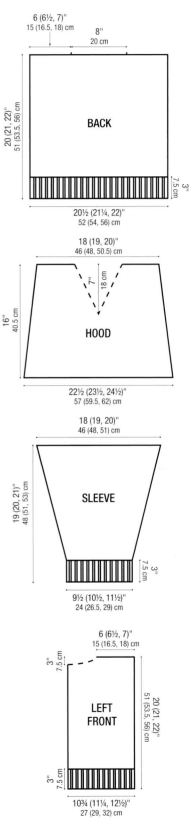

This slimming jacket is knitted in a textured rib stitch, a simple two-row pattern. The focus is a deep V-neck with a hand-crocheted or purchased button at the center.

raspberry ribs

Experience Level
Easy

Sizes
Small, Medium, Large, X-Large

Finished Bust Measurements
39 (41, 43, 45)"/99 (104, 109, 114)cm
Standard Fit

Materials
Approx total: 1250 (1375, 1500,
1625)yd/1143 (1257, 1372, 1486)m
silk and cashmere medium-weight
yarn

Knitting needles: 5mm (size 8 U.S.) *or
size to obtain gauge*

Crochet hook: 3.75mm (size F/5)

Tapestry needle for sewing seams

Gauge
20 sts and 26 rows = 4"/10cm in Rib
Stitch

Always take time to check your gauge.

Pattern Stitch
Rib Stitch
(multiple of 4 sts)

Row 1: *Knit 3, purl 1; repeat from * across.

Row 2: *Knit 2, purl 1, knit 1; repeat from * across.

Repeat rows 1 and 2 for pattern.

Instructions

BACK
Cast on 96 (100, 104, 108) sts.

Work in Rib Stitch pattern until piece measures 19 1/2 (20, 21, 22)"/49.5 (51, 53, 56)cm from beginning.

Bind off all sts in pattern for shoulders and neck.

LEFT FRONT
Cast on 48 (52, 56, 60) sts.

Work in pattern until piece measures 10½ (10¾, 10¾, 11)"/26.5 (27, 27, 28)cm from beginning.

V-neck shaping
At front edge, keeping continuity of pattern as established, decrease 1 st every 3 rows 18 (19, 22, 24) times.

Work even on remaining 30 (32, 34, 36) sts, if needed, until piece measures same as back to shoulders.

Bind off all sts in pattern.

RIGHT FRONT

Work to correspond to left front, reversing shaping.

SLEEVES

Make 2.

Cast on 48 (52, 56, 60) sts.

Work in pattern and keeping continuity of pattern, increase 1 st on each side every 6 rows 19 (19, 19, 18) times, working added sts in pattern.

Work even, if needed, on 86 (90, 94, 96) sts until sleeve measures 19 (19, 19½, 20)"/48 (48, 49.5, 51)cm from beginning.

Bind off all sts in pattern.

FINISHING

Sew shoulder seams. Mark side edges of fronts and back 8½ (9, 9¼, 9½)"/21.5 (23, 23.5, 24)cm below shoulder seams for armholes. Sew top edge of a sleeve to each side between markers. Sew underarm and side seams.

THIS PROJECT WAS KNIT WITH 10 (11, 12, 13) balls of Classic Elite Posh, 70% silk/30% cashmere yarn, medium weight, 1 3/4oz/50g = approx 125yd/114m per ball, color #93052.

Crocheted edging

With crochet hook, beginning on bottom at right seam, work a row of single crochet (sc) all around outer edges of jacket body, making a 7-chain button loop on right front at base of V-neck. Crochet a row of sc around each sleeve edge. Sew a purchased or crocheted button (see below) to left front opposite button loop.

Crocheted button

With crochet hook, chain 5 and join with slip stitch in first chain to form a ring.

Round 1: Work 7 single crochet (sc) in ring. Do not join sts, but work around and around. Mark beginning of each round.

Round 2: Work 2 sc in each sc around.

Round 3: Work sc in each sc around. Cut yarn, leaving a long end. Using tapestry needle, draw yarn through top of each st on last round and draw them tightly together. Leave button unstuffed and securely fasten off.

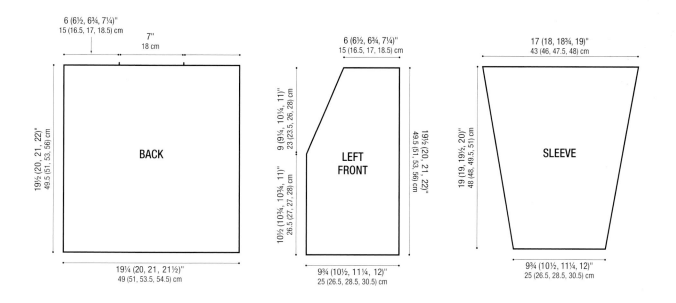

clouds

Experience Level
Very easy

Sizes
Small, Medium/Large, X-Large

Finished Bust Measurements
45½ (48, 50½)"/116 (122, 128)cm
   Loose Fit

Materials
Approx total: 546 (588, 672)yd/499
   (538, 614)m of wool super bulky-
   weight yarn

Knitting needles: 19mm (size 35 U.S.) *or
   size to obtain gauge*

Crochet hook: 6mm (size J/10)

Tapestry needle for sewing seams

Gauge
5 1/2 sts and 7 rows = 4"/10cm in
   Stockinette Stitch

Always take time to check your gauge.

This super bulky yarn is as soft and fluffy as a cloud and is perfectly suited for this long, shawl-collar coat jacket. It knits up in a very short time on extra-large needles. The simple style can be worn dressed up or down.

Pattern Stitches

Stockinette Stitch
Row 1 and all RS rows: Knit all stitches.

Row 2 and all WS rows: Purl all stitches.

Repeat rows 1 and 2 for pattern.

Garter Stitch
Knit every row.

Instructions

BACK

Cast on 30 (32, 34) sts.

Work in Stockinette Stitch until piece measures 22"/56cm from beginning.

Armhole shaping

Bind off 2 sts at beginning of next 2 rows.

Work even on 26 (28, 30) sts until piece measures 30 (31, 32)"/76 (79, 81)cm from beginning.

Bind off all sts for shoulders and neck.

LEFT FRONT

Cast on 16 (17, 18) sts.

Work in Stockinette St until piece measures same as back to armhole.

Armhole and neck shaping

At arm edge, bind off 2 sts once and at same time at neck edge, decrease 1 st every other row 6 times.

Work even on 8 (9, 10) sts until piece measures same as back to shoulders.

Bind off all sts.

RIGHT FRONT

Work to correspond to left front, reversing all shaping.

SLEEVES

Make 2.

Cast on 14 (14, 15) sts.

Work in Stockinette St, increasing 1 st each side on third row, then every 6 rows 4 (5, 5) times more.

Work even on 24 (26, 27) sts until sleeve measures 19 (19½, 20)"/48 (49.5, 51)cm from beginning.

THIS PROJECT WAS KNIT WITH 13 (14, 16) balls of Karabella *Clouds*, 100% wool yarn, super bulky weight, 3½oz/100g = approx 42yd/38m per ball.

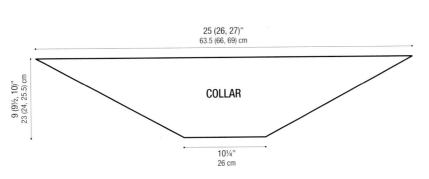

COLLAR

25 (26, 27)"
63.5 (66, 69) cm

9 (9½, 10)"
23 (24, 25.5) cm

10¼"
26 cm

Bind off all sts.

COLLAR

Cast on 14 sts.

Work in Stockinette St, increasing 1 st each side every row until piece measures 9 (9½, 10)"/23 (24, 25.5)cm from beginning.

Bind off all sts.

FINISHING

Sew shoulder seams. Sew top of a sleeve to straight armhole edge on each side, and sew top side edge of sleeves to adjacent bound-off sts of armhole. Sew underarm and side seams. Matching centers of each edge, seam longer collar edge to neck edge along back and upper fronts.

Crocheted button loop

On right front neck edge, attach yarn at point of collar and crochet a 4-chain button loop, slip stitch at base of chain, and securely fasten off. Sew a purchased or crocheted button (see below) to left front opposite button loop.

Crocheted button

With crochet hook, chain 5 and join with slip stitch to first chain to form a ring.

Round 1: Work 7 single crochet (sc) in ring. Do not join sts, but work around and around. Mark beginning of each round.

Round 2: Work 2 sc in each sc around.

Round 3: Work 1 sc in each sc around. Cut yarn, leaving a long end. Using tapestry needle, draw yarn through top of each st on last round and draw them tightly together. Leave button unstuffed and securely fasten off.

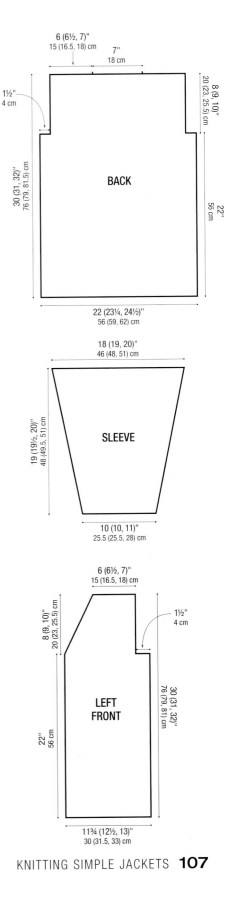

Here is an elegant variation
on a Chanel style, knit
with two strands of silk
tweed yarn held
together. The velvety
contrasting chenille
trim emphasizes
the clean lines of
this classic look.

tweed chanel

Experience Level
Easy

Sizes
Small, Medium, Large, X-Large

Finished Bust Measurements
34 (36½, 39, 41½)"/86 (93, 99,
   105.5)cm
   Standard Fit

Materials
Approx total: 1176 (1176, 1274,
   1372)yd/1075 (1075, 1165, 1255)m
   silk tweed medium-weight yarn

Approx total: 122yd/110m polyester
   chenille medium-weight yarn

Knitting needles: 6mm (size 10 U.S.) *or
   size to obtain gauge*

Crochet hook: 5mm (size H/8)

Tapestry needle for sewing seams

Gauge
11 sts and 17 rows = 4"/10cm in
   Stockinette Stitch with yarn held
   double

Always take time to check your gauge.

Pattern Stitch
Stockinette Stitch

Row 1 and all RS rows: Knit all sts.

Row 2 and all WS rows: Purl all sts.

Repeat rows 1 and 2 for pattern.

Instructions

BACK
With 2 strands of yarn held together, cast on 50 (52, 56, 58) sts.

Work in Stockinette St until piece measures 13 (13, 13½, 14)"/33 (33, 34, 35.5)cm from beginning.

Armhole shaping
Bind off 3 sts at beginning of next 2 rows.

Work even on 44 (46, 50, 52) sts until armhole is 8 (8, 8½, 9)"/20 (20, 21.5, 23)cm.

Bind off all sts for shoulders and neck.

LEFT FRONT
With yarn held double, cast on 22 (24, 26, 28) sts.

Work in Stockinette St until piece measures same as back to armholes.

Armhole shaping
At arm edge, bind off 3 sts once.

Work even on 19 (21, 23, 25) sts until armhole measures 6 (6, 6½, 7)"/15 (15, 16.5, 18)cm.

Neck shaping

THIS PROJECT WAS KNIT WITH
12 (12, 13, 14) balls of
Reynolds *Mandalay*, 100%
silk tweed yarn, medium
weight, 1¾oz/50g = approx
98yd/90m per ball, color
#39, and 1 ball of Lion
Brand Lion Suede, poly-
ester chenille yarn, medium
weight, 3oz/85g = approx
122yd/112m per ball, color #153.

At front edge, bind off 5 (6, 7, 8) sts once. Decrease 1 st at same edge every row 3 times. Work even on 11 (12, 13, 14) sts until piece measures same as back to shoulder.

Bind off all sts.

RIGHT FRONT
Work to correspond to left front, reversing all shaping.

SLEEVES
Sew shoulder seams.

With yarn held double, and right side of work facing you, pick up and knit 42 (44, 48, 50) sts along one straight armhole edge.

Beginning with a purl row on wrong side, work in Stockinette St and decrease 1 st each side every 9 (9, 8, 8) rows 8 (8, 9, 9) times. Work even on 26 (28, 30, 32) sts until sleeve measures 18½ (19, 19½, 20)"/47 (48, 49.5, 51)cm from beginning of armhole edge.

Bind off all sts.

FINISHING
Sew underarm, sleeve, and side seams.

Crocheted edging
With crochet hook and single strand of chenille, start on bottom at right seam to crochet a row of single crochet (sc) all around outer edge of jacket, working 4 sc all in same corner st to work around each lower front corner, and spacing sts to keep edges flat and smooth. When you work around to the starting point, begin working reverse sc (see Design Tip) over sts just made, working just loosely enough to keep edge smooth.

Work this same sc and reverse sc edging around each sleeve edge.

Design Tip
A reverse sc is a single crochet st worked backwards from left to right (instead of right to left) as follows:
With right side of work facing you, insert hook from front to back into the next st to the right, yarn over and draw the yarn through the st, yarn over again and draw the yarn through both loops on the hook to complete the reverse sc.

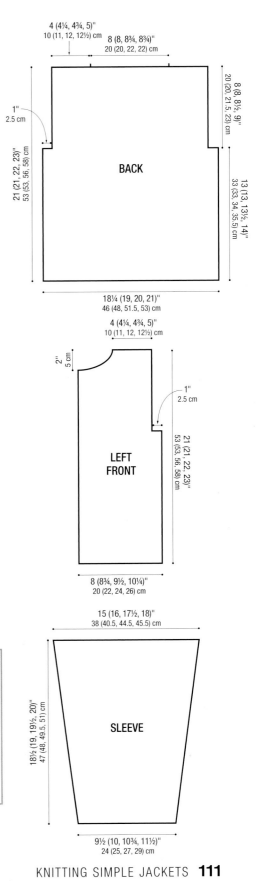

Acknowledgments

To all of you talented and generous people who helped create this book, I thank you so very, very much:

My sincere gratitude to my knitters, who completed these projects in a meticulous and professional way. This book could not have been accomplished without Jeannie Moran, Anna Alessandria, and Kathy Diekmann, all designers and long-time close friends.

The following yarn companies whose contribution of yarns for these projects is much appreciated.

Classic Elite Yarns, Galler Yarns, JCA, Inc., Karabella Yarns, Inc., Knitting Fever Inc., Muench Yarns, Inc.

The talented staff at Lark Books, whose work is first class in all respects, special thanks for your wise choices:

My editor, Linda Kopp, for her expertise, guidance, and caring throughout this detailed project.

Editor in Chief and vice president of Lark Books, Deborah Morgenthal, again, leading me gently into the beginnings of it all with grace and humor.

Stacey Budge my art director; the all-important art department for their amazing creative vision; and to Stewart O'Shields, photographer, who captured the essence of the jackets.

Ellen Liberles, technical consultant extraordinaire, who made sure that the text and diagrams are precisely correct, easy to understand, and as close to perfection as possible, a thousand thanks.

And to the models, whose natural beauty, charm, and skills add most important components to the presentation of the jacket designs.

Very important and loving thanks to my husband, Bo, who, for the initial proposal of this book, took the photos of jackets modeled by my dear daughter, Lisa, and my dear friend, Kathleen Prasad.

And last, but not least, to Carlo at Willie's Café who provided refuge by allowing me and my knitters to linger for hours in the café discussing design and knitting theory.

Index